The Kamala Harris Story

by Coen Nishiumi

Level 5

Edited by Michael Brase

JN086660

IBC パブリッシング

はじめに

　ラダーシリーズは、「はしご（ladder）」を使って一歩一歩上を目指すように、学習者の実力に合わせ、無理なくステップアップできるよう開発された英文リーダーのシリーズです。

　リーディング力をつけるためには、繰り返したくさん読むこと、いわゆる「多読」がもっとも効果的な学習法であると言われています。多読では、「1. 速く 2. 訳さず英語のまま 3. なるべく辞書を使わず」に読むことが大切です。スピードを計るなど、速く読むよう心がけましょう（たとえば TOEIC® テストの音声スピードはおよそ 1 分間に 150 語です）。そして 1 語ずつ訳すのではなく、英語を英語のまま理解するくせをつけるようにします。こうして読み続けるうちに語感がついてきて、だんだんと英語が理解できるようになるのです。まずは、ラダーシリーズの中からあなたのレベルに合った本を選び、少しずつ英文に慣れ親しんでください。たくさんの本を手にとるうちに、英文書がすらすら読めるようになってくるはずです。

《本シリーズの特徴》

- 中学校レベルから中級者レベルまで5段階に分かれています。自分に合ったレベルからスタートしてください。

- クラシックから現代文学、ノンフィクション、ビジネスと幅広いジャンルを扱っています。あなたの興味に合わせてタイトルを選べます。

- 巻末のワードリストで、いつでもどこでも単語の意味を確認できます。レベル1、2では、文中の全ての単語が、レベル3以上は中学校レベル外の単語が掲載されています。

- カバーにヘッドホーンマークのついているタイトルは、オーディオ・サポートがあります。ウェブから購入／ダウンロードし、リスニング教材としても併用できます。

《使用語彙について》

レベル1：中学校で学習する単語約1000語

レベル2：レベル1の単語＋使用頻度の高い単語約300語

レベル3：レベル1の単語＋使用頻度の高い単語約600語

レベル4：レベル1の単語＋使用頻度の高い単語約1000語

レベル5：語彙制限なし

The Kamala Harris Story

1

読みはじめる前に

【人物紹介】

Kamala Devi Harris　カマラ・デヴィ・ハリス
(1964年10月20日・カリフォルニア州オークランド生まれ)

アメリカ合衆国第49代副大統領(2021年1月20日-)で、史上初の女性・アフリカ系・アジア系の副大統領。
名門・ハワード大学を卒業後、カリフォルニア大学ヘイスティングス・ロー・スクールに学び、1990年にカリフォルニア州アラメダ郡の地方検事局でキャリアをスタートさせた。サンフランシスコ地方検事(2004-2011)、カリフォルニア州司法長官(2011-2016)の職を経て、2017年にカリフォルニア州選出の上院議員(女性として3人目)となった。2019年1月に民主党の大統領予備選挙に立候補したが、12月に撤退を表明。2020年にジョー・バイデンの副大統領候補に選出され、大統領選挙に出馬。当選を果たした。

名前の由来:

カマラ(Kamala)の名は、ヒンドゥー教の女神ラクシュミー(Lakshmi)の別名「蓮の女性(梵:bakamalā、バカマラー)」に由来する。デヴィ(Devi)も同じくサンスクリット語で「女神」の意味を持ち、ヒンドゥー教の聖なる母、偉大なる母を象徴する。

主な著書:

Smart on Crime: A Career Prosecutor's Plan to Make Us Safer (2009)
The Truths We Hold: An American Journey (2019)

家族：

父 Donald J. Harris　ドナルド・J・ハリス（1938-）
ジャマイカ人移民。カリフォルニア大学バークレー校で博士号
（経済学）を取得。1972年にはスタンフォード大学で黒人初の経
済学部教授となった（のち名誉教授）。

**母 Shyamala Gopalan Harris　シャーマラ・ゴーパーラン・
　ハリス**（1938-2009）
チェンナイ出身のタミル系インド人移民。カリフォルニア大学バ
ークレー校の動物学およびがん研究所で研究。著名な乳がん研究
者であった。

妹 Maya Harris　マヤ・ハリス（1967-）
弁護士・社会運動家・ニュース専門放送局「MSNBC」政治アナリ
スト。カリフォルニア大学バークレー校で文学士号を取得後、ス
タンフォード・ロー・スクールを卒業。2016年のアメリカ大統
領選挙では、民主党候補のヒラリー・クリントンを支える3人の
上級政策顧問の1人を務めた。

夫 Doug Emhoff　ダグ・エムホフ（1964-）
弁護士。カリフォルニア州立大学ノースリッジ校で学士号、南カ
リフォルニア大学グールド法科大学院で法務博士号を取得。前妻
との間に、コール（Cole）とエラ（Ella）の一男一女がおり、2014年
に再婚したカマラは彼らの継母となった。

When the results of the 2020 American presidential election were announced, many liberal Americans were tremendously pleased. When the news spread to India, many Indians living in Chennai, Tamil Nadu, rejoiced, for the new vice president, Kamala Harris, had ancestral roots there.

Tamil Nadu is a state located in the southernmost part of India. It is famous for its colorful Hindu temples under the bright sunshine of its tropical atmosphere. Tamil Nadu is the place where Kamala Harris has her maternal roots. Chennai is the city where her mother came from. So, for many southern Indians, the fact that Kamala was chosen to be the next US vice president was a source of pride.

On the night of November 7, 2020, Kamala Harris made a speech in front of her supporter. At the beginning of the speech, she quoted the words of John Lewis, the famous politician and civil rights activist who had recently passed way.

John Lewis had said, "Democracy is not a state. It is an act."

Kamala added, "What he meant was that America's democracy is not guaranteed. It is only as strong as our willingness to fight for it, to guard it and never take it for granted."

At that time, in front of cheering supporters, Kamala must have felt that she had found a way to protect American democracy from its enemies. She must have felt relieved that she could now heal the wounds in American life, even if many obstacles stood in the way of achieving that goal.

This statement simply represented what she had done up to the present. In reality, she had been stoutly fighting to protect the ideology of democracy, and she had been considered a woman of action. Every supporter expected her to be an active vice president who provided prompt and dynamic solutions.

What is the power of American democracy? What can the United States do for the world?

Americans commonly ask themselves these questions whenever they face a serious political event. However, it was the first time for many Americans to consider these questions while facing a crucial threat. Particularly in the four years of Donald Trump's presidency, Trump was supported by people who hated what American society had become under the influence of immigrants and minorities. Such intense feelings of division had not been felt since the Civil War ended in 1865.

The year 2020 was one of the most difficult in US history. From early spring, the country had been devastated by the pandemic. COVID-19 spread throughout the nation like wildfire. More than 20 million people contracted the deadly disease. The death toll increased day by day. People were shaken to the core by this invisible enemy.

Under such fearsome conditions, continual grievances and complaints were registered by the Black community. They insisted that Black people and minority immigrants had not been fairly treated. Above all they complained that they had not received proper care during the pandemic. These voices were particularly vocal when George Floyd, a black man, was brutally killed by white police officers in Minneapolis. The nationwide movement called "Black Lives Matter" came into being. Society was divided between those who supported it and those who opposed it.

"Black Lives Matter" is the name of the social movement against violence toward black people, particularly the outrageous and brutal treatment by local police and law enforcement officials based on racial prejudice.

The more the voices of protest spread, the greater became the counterarguments from radical white supremacists. To make things worse, in the summer and autumn forest fires wrecked destruction over the West Coast, and people argued heatedly over whether this was due to global warming based on environmental destruction caused by human beings. From the federal to the local level, people's opinions and views were split. And these splits threatened the unity of towns, schools and even families.

The tension was already palpable when Donald Trump became 45th president of the United States. He adopted a foreign policy called "America First" and promised to create a strong America by protecting the nation's interests. Based on this policy, he created a wall along with the border between the US and Mexico to restrict the illegal immigration. He also opposed environmental protection because he wanted to stimulate conventional, carbon-dioxide producing industries because he believed the protection of these industries created more jobs.

Through these policies, President Trump became the symbol of conservative Americans who were suffering from unemployment, low income, and a lack of education. Trump used Twitter to spread his message in simple language. Moreover, he condemned any news programs that were critical of him as fake news.

When George Floyd was killed, President Trump did not support the protesters standing for the black people. In fact, he denounced such protesters as left-wing radicals. As a result, he was considered an iconic figure by the extreme right wing.

On the other hand, left wing or liberal Americans were disappointed by Trump's policies and political stance. They wanted to create an open and inclusive society toward immigrants. Economically, they preferred globally connected industry. They wanted to retain American values that are tolerant of the differences among people believing in different religions, philosophies, and lifestyles. From their point of view, President Trump was nothing but a demagogue who manipulated crowds.

During the period of the election campaign, both parties were deeply damaged. Many people felt that American democracy itself was threatened. After many harsh fights, Joe Biden and Kamala Harris were eventually declared the victors. The balance of the vote was about 6 million. It was one of the most passionate elections in US history.

However, even after the heat of the election, Trump did not accept its results. He adamantly insisted that the election was rigged by liberals. As Trump's behavior became more and more radical, the tensions between Democrats and pro-Trump supporters became ever more strained.

Distrust among political opponents created as serious a scar among Americans as it had during the Civil War. Unlike the 19th century, however, the current conflict is difficult to heal because people are connected by the Internet. In the period of the Civil War, the nation was clearly divided between the states belonging to the Union and those belonging to the Confederacy.

However, current divisions are not marked by state boundaries. They are sustained by SNS, which created a web of cracks in every corner of society. The divisions have penetrated even into local communities, and even family units are not free from conflict. All over the nation, friends and colleagues became sworn enemies due to different political views. And sometimes they even became fanatical zealots.

During the election, ultra-conservative groups threatened liberal activists. They even openly carried assault weapons to express their anger and frustration. Some of them even created militia groups to attack liberal politicians.

On October 8, 2020, almost a month before the presidential election, Gretchen Whitmer,

Democratic Governor of Michigan, was on the point of being kidnapped by a radical militia group. Fortunately, the suspects were arrested before they could put their plan into action. However, this news was taken as a warning by many Americans that their democracy was on the brink of destruction.

This was the situation into which Joe Biden and Kamala Harris were elected. This was the social injury that Joe Biden and Kamala Harris needed to treat and cure. However, the task of mending a fragmented society is not an easy one. For this difficult undertaking, Kamala Harris was the emblematic figure. She is not just a vice president. She is the first female vice president, the first African American vice president, and first Asian American to be vice president.

On the night of November 7, when she spoke in front of the public celebrating the results of the election, she said, "While I may be the first woman in this office, I won't be the last."

This statement spread immediately not only throughout the United States, but also throughout the world, as words of encouragement to women who had been traditionally treated unfairly in male-oriented societies. And this statement was accepted widely as an expression of hope by the minorities who has been feeling the oppression of society.

Kamala Harris was born on October 20, 1964, the daughter of Indian and Jamaican immigrants. She is a second generation American who has pursued a political career.

Seen against this background, she is representative of the many minorities who have different roots and national origins. In one old photograph she is seen as a skinny little girl wearing long hair in braids. Around that time, together with her parents, she was already part of a group of civil right activists.

Kamala's mother, Shyamala Gopalan, came to the United States from India in 1958. At that time, it was quite demanding to travel to a nation located on the other side of the globe, where customs, living conditions, and ways of thinking were radically different. India was then a poor and developing nation. It had only become independent from the United Kingdom in 1947.

Even after independence, however, Indian society still struggled. There were serious conflicts between Hindus and Muslims. Many on both sides still followed conventional customs. Countless numbers refused to adopt a modern democratic way of life. Kamala said how difficult it was for her mother to adjust to life in the United States, a country that was thousand of miles away from her homeland and whose cultural background was so different.

When Kamala was born, Shyamala named her in association with the lotus flower, upon which typically stands the Hindu goddess Lakshmi. Kamala's mother wanted to convey to her daughter a sense of pride in her Indian background and family history.

Kamala's father, Donald J. Harris, was from Jamaica. Later he became a well-known economist after receiving a PhD from University of California, Berkeley. Kamala's parents met each other when they were attending a demonstration of civil rights movement.

After their marriage they continued to join the marches protesting the injustices against blacks and minorities. They marched with a stroller carrying Kamala. In famous story, one day when they took part in a demonstration, they found that Kamala had gotten out of the stroller and wandered off on her own.

Kamala mentioned this episode with a smile. She said, "At that time there were no seat belts on the stroller. So, I can imagine how my parents were shocked."

As this story tells us, from the beginning of her life she was familiar with the words of "freedom," "equality," and "human rights" because she heard them from her stroller while her parents marched in protest along the streets of Berkeley.

Even as a daughter of foreign-born parents, Kamala's identity has been that of an American woman of color. In 1964, and even after that, her three backgrounds as immigrant, female, and person of color could be a cause of prejudice and discrimination in American society.

Kamala's mother always considered that her daughter's fate. Therefore, from her childhood Kamala was acquainted with the notion that "democracy is an act," in the words of the famous civil rights activist John Lewis.

According to her memoir called *The Truths We Hold*, even if she was influenced by the Hindu-dominant culture of India, she often visited the Christian church belonging to the black community, where people gathered to listen to the speeches of civil rights activists. There she also studied the Bible with other black kids.

Even if she was the immigrant from India,

Shyamala believed that her children must be treated as black people in the United States. In other words, for Shyamala, what happened in the black community was her issue, too. Kamala shared this notion from the early years of her life with her younger sister, Maya.

Moreover, whenever she visited her mother's home in India, she was influenced by her grandfather, Painganadu Gopalan, who was a well-known activist for the independence of India from England. Not only Kamala's grandfather, but her grandmother also was a social activist. Above all, she worked for women's rights in India, where countless women were bound by conventional norms.

Judging from this diverse background, it is easy for us to speculate that her political stance was completely the opposite of President Trump's, who tried to close the border with Mexico by building a wall.

Kamala accepts and respects ethnic values that people have brought from all over the world. She believes that this is the strength of the United States and the backbone of US democracy. When Joe Biden became the Democratic Party's candidate in the 2020 presidential election, Kamala Harris was chosen as a stark contrast to President Trump.

2

読みはじめる前に

【アメリカと公民権の歴史】

　カマラの両親は、カリフォルニア大学バークレー校で当時行われていた公民権運動に参加したことをきっかけに知り合い、結婚しました。こうして生まれたカマラのアイデンティティや政治哲学にも深くかかわる、アメリカが歩んできた公民権の歴史をおさらいしてみましょう。

「公民権運動（Civil Rights Movement）」とは？

> 1950 ～ 60年代にかけて、主にアメリカの黒人（アフリカ系アメリカ人）が、公民権の適用と人種差別の撲滅を求めて行った大衆運動のこと。

1607年
北アメリカ大陸にイギリス領バージニア植民地が創設され、その後13の植民地が築かれる

1619年
バージニア植民地に、アフリカから「奴隷」とされる黒人を乗せた船が初めて到着する

:
イギリスやオランダなどの西欧諸国によって、アフリカ系アメリカ人や先住民族が奴隷として扱われる
:

1776年7月4日
イギリスからの「独立宣言（Declaration of Independence）」を発表。1783年のパリ条約によって、13州からなるアメリカ合衆国が正式に独立

:
19世紀の前半を通じて、奴隷制度廃止運動がアメリカ合衆国に広がる
:

1861年
南北戦争（Civil War）が勃発。北部のアメリカ合衆国23州と、奴隷制存続を主張・分離した南部のアメリカ連合国11州との間で行われる

1863年1月1日
リンカーンが「奴隷解放宣言」を発表

1865年
南北戦争が終結。アメリカ合衆国憲法修正第13条により、正式に奴隷制度が廃止される

       :
    南部諸州では、人種差別的な内容を含む「ジム・クロウ法」が次々と成立
       :

1955年
アラバマ州モンゴメリーでバス・ボイコット運動が始まる

1963年8月28日
人種差別撤廃を求めるワシントン大行進。ワシントン記念塔広場にて、キング牧師が「I Have a Dream」演説を行う

1964年7月2日
合衆国連邦議会で公民権法（Civil Rights Act）が制定される

2009年
バラク・オバマが黒人として初めて、アメリカ合衆国第44代大統領に就任（-2017）

US politics are not always easy to understand. The two main political parities are the Republican and the Democratic parties. They have different views concerning many political issues, including how to treat the immigrants flowing into the country. Immigrants and their descendants give American society variety in religion and culture. This phenomenon is called social diversity. It is also the origin of American industrial power as multitudinous seeds of knowledge come from these migrant countries.

However, Republican and Democratic supporters have different views about the value of such diversity, especially about immigrants who do not have proper documents and who have not followed due process in coming into the US. To understand this complexity, we need to study the history of American values related to civil rights, which is also deeply related to Kamala's political philosophy. Let's review the milestones of American history that have taught us how to treat people equally, including immigrants.

It is now commonly accepted that the strength of American society lies in its diversity. The majority of Americans believe this diversity has produced the productive synergy to grow their nation and communities. Throughout the history of the US, immigrants with different origins and backgrounds have been widely accepted. Actually, except for the American Indian, all Americans are immigrants or their descendants. However, it is unfortunate that this fact has often been overlooked as people were seduced by prejudice and discrimination. We can trace this negative phenomenon from the beginnings of American history.

When people arrived in the US as immi-grants, they worked hard to develop a new life. After many years they created their own property. Their desire was to have stable jobs and a safe society composed of close friends and relations.

So when newcomers arrived, the original migrants tended to obsess over whether these newcomers might threaten the privileges they had created at the cost of very hard work. Sometimes communities of immigrants fought each other for the land and privileges they had established.

Above all, there had been a long legacy of discrimination against black people, originally brought to the US as slaves.

From the beginning of its history US society has faced a challenge in this contra-diction between the ideologies of diversity and exclusive prejudice. When the United States declared their independence from the oppression of the United Kingdom, the famous document called the Declaration of Independence was declared.

This Declaration is the most frequently quoted document by politicians, philosophers, teachers, and fathers and mothers who are concerned about their children's education— particularly the globally famous "We hold these truths to be self-evident, that all men are created equal, that they are endowed by their Creator with certain unalienable Rights, that among these are Life, Liberty and the pursuit of Happiness."

However, as is widely known, when this document was announced in 1776, the people who were granted these rights were white males who owned property, which consisted largely of slaves. Even George Washington, the first president of the United States, had black slaves.

Then, in 1863, after the chaos of the Civil War, slavery was finally abolished, and countless black people were released from their former slave owners. However, this did not mean they were freed from discrimination.

In many states, even after the Civil War, black people were not treated equally with white people. They were discriminated against and even segregated.

This treatment were not only directed against black communities but applied to other new immigrants as well. For example, many Asian immigrants, including Japanese and Chinese Americans, were similarly treated as second class citizens in white-dominant America.

In the 1950s the so-called civil rights movement gained momentum. Many black leaders such as Martin Luther King Jr. demanded to share in the equal opportunities and legal rights that ordinary white citizens enjoyed.

In 1964 the government finally granted equal human rights to everyone living in the United States without exception. On July 2 1964, the Civil Rights Act came into effect. And from that time any discrimination based on race, color, religion or national origin became illegal.

1964 was also the year when Kamala Harris was born, in Oakland, California. Her parents were working at the University of California,

Berkeley, which was the birthplace of the civil rights movement.

When Kamala became an elementary schooler, she joined the school that adopted the national experiment in desegregation. It meant that schools were allowed to mix black and white students in the classroom, even if they came from neighborhoods that weren't mixed.

For the early 60s it was a very progressive experiment. In the elementary school she learned there are many people who have a different cultural holidays and languages.

It was an early stage of so-called diversity education, which is now quite popular all over the United States. However, even if it was an experimental program, this system itself was also ironically considered as a legacy of the segregation that US society had long suffered under.

"There was a little girl in California who was part of the second class to integrate her public schools. She was bused to school every day. That little girl was me."

Kamala mentioned this when she ran for president as the Democratic Party candidate. Interestingly, this statement was made during her debate with Joe Biden. It made her famous nationwide. In many cases, these experiences gave Kamala the base of her political identity.

Unfortunately, when she was 7 years old, her parents divorced. She was raised by her mother, who had a medical research job at McGill University in Montreal, Canada.

Montreal was quite a different environment from California for Kamala and Maya, her younger sister. Kamala said she missed the bright, warm sunshine of California and her friends there. She came back to her home state after she finished the course at Howard University, the famous university for black students located in Washington D.C.

After Howard she returned to Oakland and studied law. Unfortunately, she failed her first attempt at the bar exam. It was tough experience for her. It was her mother who encouraged Kamala to challenge the exam again. This time she made it.

When 26, she started her career as a public prosecutor. Her aim, she said, was to be a progressive prosecutor.

"One thing we must do is to take on the racial bias—the prejudice—in our criminal justice system. And that effort starts with our stating clearly that black lives matter—and speaking truth about what that means." (*The Truths We Hold*)

The protest movements were not only against private incidents; they were also, and particularly, against black people being treated harshly compared with other races by local police or other law enforcement agencies. Kamala wanted to change these trends from inside the public systems.

However, many people who knew Kamala questioned whether her choice of job was the right one. They thought there was a contradiction in the work of a prosecutor, whose role is to present the case in a criminal trial against an individual accused of breaking the law, while it is the defense attorney's job to represents a defendant in court proceedings.

In other words, prosecutors are lawyers who represent the state or federal government.

Many people, including Kamala, thought that the criminal system needed reform, but they thought that this would be difficult to do from within the system. Kamala, on the other hand, held that America has a deep and dark history of people using the power of the prosecutor unfairly and unjustly—"of innocent men framed, of charges brought against people of color without enough evidence, of prosecutors hiding information that would show that defendants, those charged with a crime, were innocent. I grew up with these stories—so I understood my community's suspicions. But history told another story, too." (*The Truths We Hold*)

Therefore, Kamala's decision to pursue a career as a prosecutor was quite bold and courageous.

When she decided to be a prosecutor, many of her acquaintances, including her family, were surprised. And even 20 years later, when she decided to run in the Democratic Party presidential election, some people wondered if voters would hesitate to have a presidential candidate who had a background as a prosecutor.

However, her decision was firm. She wanted to challenge the notion that the criminal system must be changed from the inside by power and authority. She said that she wanted to put herself in the position where social justice was decided. It was easy to be an attorney to defend criminals. However, she intentionally wanted to be a prosecutor and watch the mechanisms of criminal behavior and the contradictions of society.

Kamala had been thinking about "why things happen?"

When she worked as the prosecutor of Alameda County, the county near San Francisco, she was responsible for sexual offenders. Instead of just condemning their criminal behavior, she showed a strong interest in their criminal background.

She said the offenders often had similar experiences when they were children. Many criminals were themselves the victims of child abuse or sexual abuse. If so, how can they be judged guilty or innocent on the basis of such a simple notion.

It is unfair to give criminals sentences by ignoring the background that made him or her commit the crime, because in many cases there is a social contradiction or quandary behind the crimes.

That is why Kamala has been basically opposed to the death penalty. And that is what led her, after watching the development of cases that took place based on the dilemmas hidden inside society, to consider her next career, that as a politician.

As for her career as a prosecutor, she was appointed the assistant district attorney of San Francisco in 1990. And when she started her new job in there, she was involved in prosecuting the most serious crimes. She clashed with the decision of her superior who was for trying juvenile defendants in the Superior Court instead of Juvenile Courts.

Eventually she quit this job in 2000 and started working at San Francisco City Hall, handling child abuse and neglect cases. Through her career of these early years, she became known as one of the top hundred lawyers in California.

3

読みはじめる前に

【アメリカの二大政党】

アメリカは「二大政党制」の典型例とされます。現代においては、民主党と共和党がその二大政党です。二大政党の指名を受けない候補が大統領に当選した例は、19世紀以降ありません。連邦議会の議員、州知事、州議会議員、大都市の市長なども、そのほとんどが二大政党のいずれかに属しています。ここで各政党の違いを比較して、理解を深めましょう。

民主党		共和党
1828年 トマス・ジェファソン（第3代大統領）創設の民主共和党が起源とされる、世界最古の現存政党。	設立	1854年 南部奴隷制への反対勢力によって結党。党出身の初代大統領はエイブラハム・リンカーン（第16代）。
青 民主党支持層が多い州 =「blue state」 以前は「赤」だったことも。	イメージカラー	赤 共和党支持層が多い州 =「red state」 以前は「黄」だったことも。
ロバ 党所属初の大統領アンドリュー・ジャクソン（第7代）が、選挙中に共和党員から名前の「Jackson」を「jackass = ロバ（のろま・まぬけを意味する）」と揶揄されたのを逆手にとって自らのシンボルにしたのが始まりとされる。2010年には、Democratic Partyの頭文字「D」を使った新ロゴを発表。	シンボル	ゾウ 1860年の大統領選挙で、リンカーンが党の強さを象徴するために「ゾウ」を新聞に掲載したのが始まりとされる。その後、風刺画家トーマス・ナストが共和党を「ゾウ」になぞらえたことで広まったとされ、1870年代にシンボルとして採用された。別名「GOP = Grand Old Party」とも呼ばれる。

民主党		共和党
支援が必要な人たちに対して、社会福祉や生活保護を考えるのは政府の義務だとする「大きな政府」	**基本理念**	自由市場や資本主義を重視、民営化や規制緩和を推進し、政府の介入を最小限にする「小さな政府」
リベラル、国際協調、銃規制賛成、国民皆保険、環境問題、死刑廃止	**キーワード**	保守、単独行動主義、銃規制反対、移民の制限、中絶反対、親イスラエル
大都市が集まる東海岸や西海岸 女性、大卒者、ミレニアル世代、性的・宗教的・人種的マイノリティー	**支持基盤**	中西部の農業地域や南部 白人男性、福音派キリスト教徒
バラク・オバマ（第44代） ビル・クリントン（第42代） ジミー・カーター（第39代） ジョン・F・ケネディ（第35代） フランクリン・ルーズベルト（第32代）	**主な歴代大統領**	ドナルド・トランプ（第45代） ジョージ・W・ブッシュ（第43代） ジョージ・H・W・ブッシュ（第41代） ロナルド・レーガン（第40代） リチャード・ニクソン（第37代）

Traditionally, the State of California is a strong base of the Democratic Party. As everybody knows, Kamala Harris also belongs to the Democratic Party.

Americans consider the Democratic Party to be liberal and progressive, while the Republican Party stands for the conservative side. Now, to understand Kamala's political views, we need to understand what is liberal and what is conservative for Americans.

To do this, let's go back to the era when the United States was formed. When the United States fought for their independence, people were united behind the mutual goal of achieving victory against the United Kingdom. However, because America consisted of countless settlers (mainly from Europe), the concept and identity of America as a tightly united nation was not strong enough to create a centralized government.

They came to this new world for various reasons some came to escape from poverty. Some wanted a safe place to live; they had been oppressed in their home countries for political, religious, or other reasons. And some came to the new world to seek profit or business opportunities.

They settled down to cultivate the new land They traded with native Americans. Some of them started new businesses. These settlers were bound together in order to protect themselves and to create their own rules to run their villages or towns.

Therefore, after independence, even if the nation needed federal law and a federal tax system, there were still many conflicts of interest between the individual settlers.

However, to create a new country, a new government needed to enforce federal systems with strong law enforcement. The problem was how to compromise with each settler, region, and state so that they could accept the laws and systems that the new federal government would create.

Thus they decided to give strong independent power to local government while assigning the federal government and constitution the power of diplomacy, military action, and executive power.

First of all, a new tax system was needed to finance the federal government, adding another burden to the people's expenses. Consequently, it took years' of strident argument and conflict to create the system of federal government.

This is the reason why Americans are generally quite sensitive about how their taxes are used. Simultaneously, every state has their own constitution and judicial power. Every state can make their own decision for their administrative strategies.

This system remains in effect even today. In Kamala's case, she was working under the legal system of state of California, which has its own law and constitution.

The states of the United States of America have long managed to maintain this balance between the federal and the local. In other words, Americans have been discussing and arguing how the federal government can execute its power in local areas since the beginning of their history.

In the 19th century the argument was developed that all states should follow the lead of the federal government. At issue was the question of whether the slavery system could be abolished by federal law throughout the entirety of the United States.

In the middle of 19th century, America was divided between the states that stood for slavery and those that stood against it.

Eventually, the Southern States, which chose to maintain slavery, created the Confederate States of America to be independent from the federal government. This was the cause of the Civil War fought between 1861 and 1865.

The Civil War was a typical example of how local governments can resist the lead of the federal government. In this case, the federal government under the leadership of President Abraham Lincoln tried to abolish the slavery system because he and his supporters believed it to be inhuman.

However, many Southern States considered Lincoln's proposals an infringement of their power and freedom. Therefore, they decided to withdraw from the unity of the federal government and establish the Confederacy.

The ensuing Civil War created a nationwide struggle of immense proportions. Fortunately, the Union or Federal government defeated the Confederacy. Even after the end of war, however, the arguments related to local autonomy versus federal domination have continued unabated.

Some people think federal power should be small and limited. If small and limited, they believe they can enjoy greater freedom and pay less taxes. Currently, many cases are still on the political table waiting to see if they fall under the control of federal law or not. Typical examples are gun control and national health insurance.

In the era of the early pioneers, every settler needed to possess weapons for protection. When people originally stood up in the name of independence, they formed militia bearing their own weapons.

However, now many people consider that tradition to be out of date. They insist that the legal right to bear arms should be banished. They point to the countless brutal crimes committed by people possessing assault weapons.

The Democratic Party, including Kamala Harris, is traditionally in sympathy with those who oppose bearing arms. On the other hand, many Republicans insist that the possession of a gun is an individual choice, not an issue in which the federal government should intervene. Some people even champion the gun as a symbol of freedom.

The argument for and against national health insurance is based on similar thinking. Generally, Democrats insist on stronger federal government, while Republicans prefer smaller government.

Democrats argue that in order to save the less wealthy, an insurance system that cover the entire nation is needed. The Republican's counterargument is that this will causes the federal government to grow bigger and stronger. As it gets bigger, people will have to pay more taxes to sustain it. Politicians belonging to the Republican Party abhor this idea. When COVID-19 began to spread all over the country, this argument began to sound heartless because many people fighting the pandemic were not rich enough to protect themselves.

When Joe Biden served as the vice president of the Obama administration between 2008 and 2016, the Affordable Care Act, or so-called Obama Care, was finally signed into law. After Donald Trump became president, he tried to abolish this system, to delegate each aspect of the system to local or private sectors. Now COVID-19 has killed almost a half million Americans, both rich and poor. Everybody knows the virus attacks people indiscriminately.

Therefore, Kamala Harris's first and most important job as vice president was to tackle this pandemic. She may even need to renovate Obama Care to benefit every American citizen. In other words, she will try to revitalize the system so that it allows all people to get the same treatment under the cover of the insurance plan.

She was the main supporter of Obama Care. And now she needs to even enrich the quality of the system to wipe this cruel disease from the face of the United States, even if there is a persistent resistance from conservative Americans who want to keep a small government.

4

読みはじめる前に

【バイデン大統領と民主党】

　カマラを大統領選挙とその後の政権運営の伴走者 (running mate) に選んだ、バイデン大統領。その選択の背景には、どのような事情があったのでしょうか。ここでは、彼の政治的立場や民主党の内情を整理してみましょう。

Joe Biden　ジョー・バイデン
（1942年11月20日・ペンシルベニア州スクラントン生まれ）

アメリカ合衆国第46代大統領 (2021年1月20日–) で、ジョン・F・ケネディ以来2人目のカトリックの大統領。就任時の年齢 (78歳) は史上最高齢。弁護士としてキャリアをスタート後、ニューキャッスル郡議会議員、デラウェア州選出上院議員を経て、バラク・オバマ政権で第47代副大統領を歴任。

《政治的立場》
・民主党「中道派」の重鎮であり、政治的・思想的に偏りが少ない
・アイルランド系カトリックであるため、白人労働者やカトリックの支持が強い
・上院外交委員長として外交経験が豊富で、国民にも "外交通" として認知されている

　2016年と2020年の大統領選予備選挙など、近年の民主党内では中道派と左派の対立が際立ってきている。党の大統領候補者指名争いで、クリントン氏およびバイデン氏と最後まで激戦をくり広げたサンダース氏は、みずからを「社会民主主義者」と呼び、熱狂的な若者を中心に幅広い支持を得た。

　アメリカは20世紀を通じてソ連率いる社会主義国と対峙してきたことから、多くのアメリカ人、特に中南米からの移民が多い地域では「社会主義」に対する抵抗感が強い。共和党から「民主党

＝社会主義勢力」のレッテルを貼られることを忌避し、何よりも打倒トランプ（共和党）を目指した結果、女性やマイノリティーからの支持も得られるカマラに白羽の矢が立ったとされる。

民主党内の「中道派」と「左派」って？

●中道派（中道左派・穏健派）

急進的・反動的な政策に反対ないし慎重な立場をとり、穏健的な政策を主張する勢力のこと。イデオロギー（観念や思想）ではなく現実主義的で、議会制民主主義や少数意見の尊重など公正な思想・姿勢を指す。

⇒ジョー・バイデン、カマラ・ハリス、ヒラリー・クリントン、ピート・ブティジェッジ、バラク・オバマなど

●左派（急進左派）

革新的・急進的な政策を主張する勢力のこと。「より平等な社会を目指すための社会変革を支持する層」で、革命的な政治勢力や人を指すこともあり、社会主義的、共産主義的な傾向が見られる。

⇒バーニー・サンダース、エリザベス・ウォーレン、アレクサンドリア・オカシオ＝コルテスなど

主な論点

・国民皆保険制度の導入

・黒人暴行事件の多発を受けた、警察の解体や予算削減

・格差改善のための最低賃金引き上げ

・社会保障財源に充てる、大企業や富裕層からの「富裕税」の取り立て

・「グリーンニューディール」

　→自然エネルギーや地球温暖化対策に公共投資することで、新たな雇用や経済成長を生み出す政策

Given this historical background, let's take a look at the presidential election of 2020. Before the election campaign started, Kamala Harris was already one of the most influential senators in the Democratic Party.

Throughout her career as a senator, she actively targeted her opponents and questioned them at public hearings.

Through these events, her skillful presentation and reasoning, based on her experience as a prosecutor, was highly appreciated both by Democrats and Republicans.

She is without doubt a logical thinker. Whenever she presents an argument in public, she always makes her point by showing the "basis" and "reason" of the point she wants to initiate.

As everybody knows, people tend to become emotional when they complain. If a person wants to protest strongly against an unfairness, his or her voice may become strong, loud, and harsh.

Kamala's attitude is different, however. Even though she may prefer to present a strong argument in a tough voice, she is always cool in challenging situations or when condemning others. At the same time, she hates to leave problems half-solved or to compromise when she considers something wrong. She is a tough negotiator, though her appearance belies it.

After serving three years as a senator, many people expected she would be one of the candidates in the upcoming 2020 presidential election, which she eventually was. In time, however, she dropped out of the race for the presidency and endorsed Joe Biden as the for-mal candidate of Democratic Party.

Basically, Joe Biden had placed himself in the middle of the road within the Democratic Party. His most serious rival for the Democratic nomination as president was Bernie Sanders, referred to as the super left of the Democratic Party.

It would have been highly interesting if Sanders and President Trump had contended for the ticket to the next White House resident because their way of thinking is diametrically opposite. Many people who consider themselves to be "quite liberal" expected Sanders be nominated. Particularly he had many supporters in California, Vermont, and other major states where the Democratic party traditionally had a strong base. However, as the result of internal competition, Biden eventually got the ticket for the election.

Many Americans were concerned that Biden was too moderate to fight against President Trump, who had a strong character. Also, Biden was already 78 years old. If he became president, he would be the oldest president in US history. People automatically worried about his health and whether he could remain strong during his term in office.

To win the election, Biden was expected to face tough debates and rough campaigns. Also, even though many people had already admitted that Trump was a populist, it was true that he was good at talking to voters in simple, strong and seductive language. Trump's talented self-promotion attracted many voters, even among the so-called swing states.

Plus, for Democrats and liberals in general, it was feared that Trump could promote his actual performance as president through the media. Therefore, everybody expected it would be a tough race.

If that turned out to be the case, Biden could not lose the support of the super liberals or minority immigrant voters inside the swing states.

These are the reasons that Biden chose Kamala Harris as his running mate. When Biden made the announcement, some journalists called it the great "hidden ball trick."

So, for Joe Biden, Kamala Harris was the

perfect person for the upcoming election: she was the daughter of Indian and Jamaican immigrants, was considered black herself, and had had a brilliant background as the government prosecutor based on a quite liberal ideology. Plus, there was another reason that Joe Biden chose Kamala as his running mate.

When Kamala was California's Attorney General in 2011, she fought to protect the many poor house owners from the big financial firms. The US was suffering from a serious recession.

Due to the economic crisis that started in 2008, many house owners defaulted on their mortgages. Then, around 2011, countless people were facing the threat of foreclosure.

When she tried to protect those people, Beau Biden, Joe Biden's son, supported her effort. At that time, Beau Biden was the Attorney General of Delaware.

Both supported each other and shared information on how to fight against the banks who created mortgage schemes for the low-income families.

As the result of the teamwork between Kamala and Beau, Kamala could get better settlements for the people fearful of losing their homes by creating a special salvation act to fund relief for needy homeowners.

So it came as a shock in 2015 when Kamala learned that Beau Biden had died due to a brain tumor. Thus, through Kamala's friendship with Beau, Joe Biden evaluated Kamala highly even before he chose her for his running mate in the 2020 presidential election.

In August 17, 2020, the National Convention of the Democratic Party was held in Milwaukee, Wisconsin. It was there that the final and formal announcement was made that Joe Biden and Kamala Harris were to be the Democratic Party candidates of for the upcoming election.

However, some Democratic Party members

were concerned that Kamala was too liberal and that she might create division within the party. Some pointed out what happened when she was the San Francisco district attorney.

Kamala was serving as the district attorney of San Francisco between 2004 and 2011 as the result of the election of 2003. Almost immediately after her appointment, she had to take on the case of a local police officer who was murdered while on duty.

On the night of April 10 in 2004, Isaac Espinoza, a young San Francisco police officer was shot and killed when he and his partner were patrolling a high crime area of the city.

It happened when Officer Espinoza questioned a suspicious person who seemed to hide something in his coat. When Espinoza approached the suspect, he instantly fired an assault rifle and killed Officer Espinoza.

After the police officer's death, the suspect was arrested. His name was David Hill, a member of a local gang. The area where

Officer Espinoza was patrolling was notorious for its criminal activity, including rape, murder, narcotic sales and more.

David Hill was apparently a member of a gang that had been involved in crimes that threatened the neighborhood and community. Since the state of California has the death penalty for crimes of this seriousness, everyone expected the prosecutor to seek the death sentence for David Hill.

However, the case occurred immediately after Harris's election as San Francisco district attorney; she announced in a press conference that she would not seek capital punishment.

It was an unexpected announcement.

"So soon after the death. I wanted to be active on that case—not based on the emotion based on the fact and law," she said in the press conference.

Controversy erupted at the funeral. When the victim's families were crying for the death penalty, standing ovation attacked Kamala who was also attended.

The police officers who lost their colleague, and even some politicians belonging to the Democratic Party, opposed her decision because nobody could find a mistake the victim had made when he tried to enforce the law. In fact, Officer Espinoza was liked by his colleagues and the local community as well.

As for Kamala, she had been against the death penalty from the beginning of her legal career.

Above all, when Kamala decided to run for the seat of district attorney of San Francisco in 2003, she pledged that she would not seek the death penalty for any case. Her decision against David Hill was based on that pledge.

She considers finding the story behind the crime more important than executing the criminal. So in many cases in which she was prosecutor she asked that criminals who had committed serious crimes be sentenced to life imprisonment without parole.

So she did same with David Hill.

For Kamala, it was more important for serious offenders to pay for what they had done by spending all of their life in jail rather than just executing them.

However, some people considered this ideology is to be an individual ideology. They thought she should not mix her personal ideology with the existent legal system. Some people insisted as far as death penalty was legally granted in the criminal law of the state of California, the punishment called for what David Hill did was appropriate in this case.

Indeed, this was the center of the controversy. However, her liberal stance was widely accepted in the Bay Area.

As for the black community, Kamala thinks that it is likely to continue to face unfair treatment by law enforcement officers. In the US, racial bias has always become an issue whenever black people come into contact with local police.

According to Kamala the root cause is the

prejudice in the US criminal justice system. And that complaint has developed the strong movement called "Black Lives Matter."

In her book *The Truths We Hold*, Kamala cites statistics across the nation that show when a police officer stops a black driver, he is three times more likely to search the car than when the driver is white. Kamala also insists that black men use drugs at the same rate as white men, but they are arrested twice as often for it. As a result, black men are six times as likely as white men to be jailed. And when they are convicted, black men get prison sentences nearly 20 percent longer than those given to white men who committed the same crime.

She has had a deep sympathy with such unfairness. When working in San Francisco, she created a special education system for narcotic offenders, many of whom were black.

The plan called for these people to be provided education at the same level as a high school graduate. Almost all offenders participating in this special education program did not return to a life of crime.

"We need to give them the resources for the criminal offender to have a better life," once she said in the press conference.

5

読みはじめる前に

【アメリカ大統領選挙のしくみ】

　カマラの妹マヤは2016年のアメリカ大統領選挙で、民主党候補のヒラリー・クリントンを支える上級政策顧問の1人でした。しかし結果は、共和党候補のドナルド・トランプが勝利。クリントン氏の方が総得票数は上回っていたはずなのに、選挙に敗北したのはどうしてでしょうか。日本とは異なるアメリカの選挙について、知っておきましょう。

開催	4年に1度（近年では夏季オリンピック・パラリンピックと同じ年）
任期	大統領および副大統領は4年の任期を務める
選挙権	事前に自己申告で登録を行った、18歳以上のアメリカ国籍者に与えられる（永住権者は該当しない）
被選挙権	下記の要件を満たしている者に与えられる ・35歳以上であること ・アメリカ合衆国内で出生したアメリカ合衆国市民であること（両親がアメリカ国籍であれば、国外で出生しても構わない） ・14年以上アメリカ合衆国内に居住している 　大統領に3度選出されること、昇格や職務代行により2年以上大統領の職務を行った人物が複数回大統領に選出されることは禁止されている。多くの州では二大政党（民主党と共和党）以外からの立候補に、一定数の有権者による署名を必要としており、第三勢力の候補者は署名が揃わず、一部の州でしか立候補できない事例が多い。
投票日	連邦法の規定により、有権者が大統領候補者に票を投じる「一般投票」は「11月第1月曜日の翌日の火曜日」に、その後「12月第2水曜日の次の月曜日」に各州で選挙人団が集会し「選挙人投票」が行われる。

「選挙人（elector）」とは？

大統領選挙の選挙人集会で、大統領および副大統領を選出する人のこと。州ごとに人口に応じて、連邦上下両院の合計議席と同じ数で割り当てられ、その総数は538名となる。

投票は州ごとに行われ、ほとんどの州で、勝者がその州の選挙人をすべて獲得する「勝者総取り方式」を採用。例えば、カリフォルニア州で勝者となった候補は、割り当てられた選挙人55名すべてを獲得する。

そして、全米538名の選挙人のうち、過半数の270名以上を獲得した候補が最終的な勝者、つまり次期大統領・副大統領となる。

2016年の大統領選挙では、民主党のクリントン氏が総得票数で200万票以上も多かったが、選挙人の数では共和党のトランプ氏が306名を獲得したため、トランプ氏の勝利・大統領就任となった。

Kamala's firm stance and ideology concerning crime was apparently based on the education given by her parents, who were active in the Civil Rights movement. And we cannot forget her younger sister, Maya's, role. Maya and Kamala exercised a strong influence on one another.

Maya, as a famous law school professor, supported Kamala's every move. Maya also became one of the most important strategists for Hillary Clinton in the 2016 presidential election.

Before becoming a US senator, she served as attorney general of California between 2011 and 2017. She was the first black, first woman, and first person of Asian background for that position.

When she was the district attorney of San Francisco between 2004 and 2011, she was involved in many legal reforms, including opposition to the death penalty, promotion of same sex marriage, and so on.

Based on her progressive background and performance as the district attorney of San Francisco, she was elected attorney general of California.

It was the time of the presidency of Barack Obama. Many people expected that the US would become more liberal under the leadership of country's first black president. However, things were not so simple.

When society is going to change, there are always scapegoats. Many are right-wing people, particularly white people, and above all white male blue-collar workers, who had been targeted as the most conservative. Their frustration had accumulated partly because of their poor economic situation. They considered immigrants and the new liberal ways of thinking as destroying their traditional values. They thought they must regain the good old American lifestyle that diligent "white Christians" had created.

In addition, they believed they needed to protect their jobs from workers coming from abroad. Above all, they hated any intervention from the federal government. They wanted to maintain their way of life in their local homeland.

When their frustration had come to a head, Donald Trump appeared. Donald Trump promised that he would give them relief. He said he would give American interests top priority. It was 2016 when Donald Trump was elected as the 45th president of the United State by defeating Hillary Clinton, who many expected would be a first female president.

Accordingly, after Obama's administration was concluded, the pendulum of US politics swung in the opposite direction.

After Trump was elected president, he withdrew the US from the Paris Agreement, the international agreement to protect the planet by reducing greenhouse gas emission.

Throughout the election campaign, Mr. Trump mentioned the concept of "America First." He promised that he would be tough on imports to protect American workers and products.

Based on this policy he targeted China by imposing heavy import tariffs. The tension between the two counties mounted. He also emphasized that he would save Americans from poverty by excluding immigrants.

Kamala was elected as a US senator right before Donald Trump became the president of the United States. Of course, it was a shocking moment for many Democrats, including Kamala, that Trump defeated Hillary Clinton, even though Hillary won the popular vote.

They expected Trump's tough stance against the minority immigrants. They expected that he would radically challenge any policies that President Obama had created.

One of the most disappointed was Kamala's

sister, Maya, who formally supported Ms.
Clinton as one of the main strategists for the
campaign.

Therefore Kamala decided to fight for any
unfairness against the immigrants and minorities under the Trump administration.

She said, "We will fight, simple."

As a matter of course, it became her first
job as a senator to protect immigrants. She
insisted that undocumented immigrants are not
criminals. It might be true that there are many
immigrants living in the US without proper
authorization. For example, the immigrants
who came to the US for economic reasons may
not have working permits. However, to support
their families or simply to survive, they try to
find work. Or many immigrants have come
across the Mexican border without proper pro-
cessing. They are generally referred to as illegal
immigrants, and formally they are categorized
as undocumented immigrants.

Kamala believes even if they do not have

proper documents to support their status, they do have human rights. They are not criminals.

Above all, she strongly believes that the children of such immigrants must be protected under US law. As the daughter of immigrant parents, she understands why people come to the US in pursuit of their dreams. As in the past, they were trying to escape poverty, the dangers of society, and the politics of their mother countries. Especially, when Kamala held public office in California, she witnessed how immigrants from central American countries needed help.

She realized before the election that President Trump would be hard on immigrants, especially undocumented immigrants. He particularly tried to create the wall along the Mexican border to stop people coming into the US without being properly interviewed by immigration officers.

At one time, hundreds and thousands of desperate immigrants traveled on foot from the countries of Central America all way to the

US through Mexico. For them, if a wall were completed to push them back, it would be a matter of life or death.

The media reported tragic incidents that happened among such immigrants. They reported the death of a poor and weak child in the detention center at the border. There were similar cases, some occurring even before the term of President Trump. Immigrant parents were often separated from their children without proper reason. The immigration system was not well coordinated between the system and the human rights of the people caught at the detention centers.

Kamala has been trying hard to rectify these problems.

During Trump's term of presidency, there were serious issues concerning the immigrant children raised in the US. They were on the brink of deportation even if they had been living their entire lives in the United States. As a senator, Kamala tried to save these people by supporting the creation of the DREAM Act.

The DREAM Act is a legal proposal to protect the children of undocumented immigrants to stay and receive an education in the US. If they achieve this goal, they can become permanent residents.

This proposal was jeopardized under the Trump administration.

Also, due to the September 11 attacks in 2001, anti-Muslim sentiment had been growing in America.

At the beginning of the Trump administration, he issued an executive order banning travel to the US from Muslim countries. In the early days of her career as a senator, Kamala strongly condemned President Trump for this. She even called White House chief of staff John Kelly at his home and questioned him to gather information. Eventually, she played an important role in pushing back this order as "unconstitutional."

However, Kamala and many Democrats were concerned about a possible shift in the court's decision when the balance of power in the Supreme Court changed.

As everybody knows, creating law is the job of the Congress. And the Supreme Court can judge if such a law or presidential executive order is constitutional. The risk is that the judges of the Supreme Court are appointed by the president and must be approved by the senate. At that time, Republicans held the majority in the senate. The tenure of a Supreme Court Judge is lifetime. So once a judge dies, a new judge must be appointed. That is the job of the president, who nominates a new Supreme Court Judge.

During the term of President Trump, the balance of the Supreme Court Judges leaned toward the conservative side. So Kamala Harris and her colleagues were deeply concerned about the trend toward anti-immigration.

She remembered how her mother, an Indian immigrant, raised her and her sister. Her mother passed away in 2009 due to the colon cancer.

Again, due to the influence of her mother and father, the protection of the human rights of immigrants and minorities became Kamala's lifetime task; she believes that freedom and equality must be given to people in every corner of American society.

There is little doubt that the time from 2016 onward, when Trump was elected president, was a dark period for Kamala. She received countless telephone calls from lawyers and supporters of poor immigrants who were in danger of losing their status.

In 2018, as the result of the middle term election, Democrats regained a majority in the House of Representatives.

It was the first successful counterattack by the liberal side against Donald Trump. However, the Senate, of which Kamala was a member, was still occupied by Republicans as the majority party. Therefore, the presidential election of 2020 was a critically important election for both sides.

6

読みはじめる前に

【アメリカの2020年とこれから】

　2020年から始まった新型コロナウイルスの世界的な大流行（パンデミック）によって、今まさに私たちは時代の転換点に立っています。そして、アメリカ国内にとどまらず世界中から大きな関心が寄せられた、歴史的な大統領選挙を制したジョー・バイデンとカマラ・ハリス。この二人がこれからどのような舵取りを行っていくのか、注目していきましょう。

★新型コロナウイルス（COVID-19）の感染拡大

　2020年1月20日にアメリカ国内で初の感染者が確認されて以来、累計の感染者数は33,026,624名、死者数は587,874名（2021年5月19日現在）。外食産業を筆頭に、余暇・娯楽業を中心とした失業者の増加、雇用の落ち込みが課題となっている。ワクチン接種の迅速な拡大により、経済活動を再開する動きも本格化しており、ワクチン接種が完了している人に対するマスク着用の緩和も進めている。

★# Black Lives Matter, # Stop Asian Hate

　2020年には「Black Lives Matter（黒人の命は大切）」をスローガンとする全米的なデモ・暴動が広がりを見せた。2020年5月25日、アフリカ系アメリカ人男性のジョージ・フロイドが、ミネソタ州ミネアポリス近郊で白人警察官の不適切な拘束によって殺害された事件を発端に、人種による不平等な扱いへの不満が紛糾した。

　そして、2021年に入ってからは「Stop Asian Hate（アジア系へのヘイトをやめよう）」の呼びかけが広がっている。トランプ前大統領が新型コロナウイルスを「チャイナウイルス」と呼んだことから、アジア系へのヘイトクライムが急増。改めてアメリカ社会の分断、人種差別の根深さが浮き彫りになった。

★パリ協定（Paris Agreement）への復帰

　パリ協定は、2015年12月12日に第21回気候変動枠組条約締約国会議（COP21）が開催されたフランス・パリで採択された。産業革命前からの世界の平均気温上昇を「2℃未満」に抑え、平均気温上昇「1.5℃未満」を目標として、各締約国が削減目標を作成・提出・維持し、目的を達成するための国内対策をとる義務を負う。アメリカは「2025年までに、2005年比で温室効果ガス排出量の26～28％削減に向けて最大限の努力をする」としている。

　2017年6月1日に、当時のトランプ大統領は離脱の意向を示した（2019年11月4日正式に離脱）。「アメリカ第一主義」を掲げるトランプ氏は地球温暖化に懐疑的で、製造業の競争力を削ぐ不公平な協定だと主張した。2021年1月20日、大統領に就任したバイデン氏は、初執務としてパリ協定復帰を含む17本の大統領令に署名・発効。クリーンエネルギーや環境インフラへの設備投資を掲げるなど、気候変動政策の軌道修正を急いでいる。

Until the beginning of 2020, many people expected that President Trump would be re-elected because history shows that an incumbent candidate always has a strong advantage. However, in February the situation started to change.

When COVID-19 started to spread, people condemned the slow action of the federal government in protecting the nation. The Trump administration was reluctant to promote wearing masks, even though many professionals repeatedly encouraged their use.

Society itself was divided between people who believed in science and those who didn't. Many Trump supporters hated to wear masks under the mandate of the government. They insisted that it should be a matter of free choice.

Too many people this argument has a strange ring, because masks are not an ideology but just a means of protecting people against a virus. Nevertheless, masks became the political insignia setting off liberals and conservatives.

Unfortunately, COVID-19 spread so rapidly that American society was devastated by an unbelievable number of deaths. And in October 2020, even President Trump was diagnosed with COVID-19.

Up to January 20 when Joe Biden became the president of the United States, more than 400,000 deaths were recorded, which is more than the total number of US soldiers deaths in World War II.

While people were suffering from the pandemic, an unforgettable atrocity occurred against a black person that would change society.

On May 25, 2020, George Floyd was brutally killed by a police officer in Minneapolis. Floyd died due to suffocation when an officer knelt on Floyd's neck for more than eight minutes. Floyd was suspected of passing a counterfeit

$20 bill. Even as Floyd desperately said, "I can't breathe," the policeman did not ease the pressure on his neck.

This case ignited nationwide movement called Black Lives Matter.

When people marched near the White House in protest, the police crushed the protesters. This use of force was severely criticized by the media since the demonstration was a peaceful one.

In addition, due to the dry and hot weather, forest fires in summer and autumn destroyed countless properties in California, Oregon, and Washington. Even though President Trump blamed the states for poor protection against fires, it was clear that much of the nation's forestlands were the territory of the federal government. The forest fires were not seen as just a natural disaster. They were taken as the result of the policy of Donald Trump, who had ignored the threat of global warming.

The process of selecting a new president

is fought state by state. The candidate who receives the most votes in a state will be the victor in that state and the winner of all the electors possessed by that state. The electors from all states make up the electoral college. The college votes to decide who will be the next president. The number of electors in the electoral college is based on the population of each state.

The election of 2020 was done both by mail-in and in-person voting due to COVID-19. The end result was that Joe Biden and Kamala Harris got more electoral college votes than President Trump.

Due to fears for the future and for division within the nation, as well as the desire to overcome COVID-19, voter turnout reached a record high. At the final stages of the vote counting, everybody closely watched the results in Pennsylvania, Georgia and Arizona.

Pennsylvania is known as a typical swing state, where people voted for Donald Trump last time. Georgia and Arizona are traditionally strong bases for Republicans.

Good news arrived a few days later: all three states had been won by Biden and Harris. Another state people were waiting for was Nevada, which leaned slightly toward the Democratic Party. Eventually, Joe Biden and Kamala Harris received 306 electoral colleges while President Trump received 232.

The total individual vote, or popular vote, was 81,283,485 for Biden and Harris. The people voting for Trump totaled 74,223,744.

It was a momentous victory.

Both Joe Biden and Kamala Harris know that there is a tremendous amount of work awaiting them. The immediate issue is to rid the US of COVID-19 and recover from the economic damage brought on by the pandemic.

The United States will also need to find a way to make its presence felt to he world. That includes how to achieve a balance of power with China. While President Trump was in charge, there was serious tension between the two powers over economic and political matters related to Hong Kong and the security of Far Eastern and South Eastern Asia. Rebuilding the relationship with the European Community is also important. Trump's "America First" policy was not welcomed by major European countries.

Biden and Harris need to make a change in environment policy by working with major nations to save the planet by supporting clean gas. Most importantly, they need to heal the wounds that have so seriously divided the American people.

Protecting American democracy is a serious task for the entire world, not just the United States. The divisions between the rich and the poor, urban and rural, educated and uneducated have grown ever wider. The distrust between people belonging to ethnic groups and majorities became the seeds of political conflict.

There is no dispute that can be remedied overnight. However, when Kamala was born, she was ready to inherit this healing ideology from her parents. There is no doubt that she has the genes to do good as the vice president of the United State.

Politics needs compromise.

Society is not simple. And now the United State is hurting from this complexity.

Kamala's name itself holds out hope for the future. It means "Lotus Flower."

The lotus is a symbol for many Asian goods and mythological beings coming to save people with their power and knowledge.

The lotus is a symbol of mercy and affection.

The lotus flower shows the salvation of the people beyond "good or bad" symbolized by the "Lady of Justice with a balance scale" standing in front of many courthouses.

The United State needs to heal itself and recover its strength by integrating every citizen's unique power. This is done by compromise in the face of difference and intolerance.

The question is, can the concept of the

6

lotus that is inherited from Asia compromise the Lady of Justice? This is the real task for Kamala Harris, who herself is an example of the diversity of America. Everyone expected her to be a proactive, energetic, and determined vice president.

Here, below, is a copy of her statement made on Saturday night of November 7—seventy-four days before she formally became the vice president of the United States. The place was Wilmington, Delaware. It was her victory speech.

Kamala appeared in front of an audience with her husband, Doug Emhoff, who she married in 2014 while the attorney general of the state of California.

Doug was an entertainment lawyer. Since this was his second marriage, Kamala became the stepmother of his two children. They called her Momala, "mother Kamala."

After concluding her speech with a smile

87

and a cheerful wave, she introduced Joe Biden as the new president-elect.

November 7 Statement

Good evening.

Congressman John Lewis, before his passing, wrote: "Democracy is not a state. It is an act."

And what he meant was that America's democracy is not guaranteed.

It is only as strong as our willingness to fight for it, to guard it and never take it for granted.

And protecting our democracy takes struggle.

It takes sacrifice. There is joy in it and there is progress.

Because 'We The People' have the power to build a better future.

And when our very democracy was on the ballot in this election, with the very soul of America at stake, and the world watching, you ushered in a new day for America.

To our campaign staff and volunteers, this extraordinary team—thank you for bringing more people than ever before into the democratic process and for making this victory possible.

To the poll workers and election officials across our country who have worked tirelessly to make sure every vote is counted—our nation owes you a debt of gratitude as you have protected the integrity of our democracy.

And to the American people who make up our beautiful country—thank you for turning out in record numbers to make your voices heard.

I know times have been challenging, especially the last several months.

The grief, sorrow, and pain. The worries and the struggles.

But we've also witnessed your courage, your resilience, and the generosity of your spirit.

For 4 years, you marched and organized for equality and justice, for our lives, and for our planet.

And then, you voted. You delivered a clear message.

You chose hope, unity, decency, science, and, yes, truth.

You chose Joe Biden as the next president of the United States of America.

Joe is a healer. A uniter. A tested and steady hand.

A person whose own experience of loss gives him a sense of purpose that will help us, as a nation, reclaim our own sense of purpose.

And a man with a big heart who loves with abandon.

It's his love for Jill, who will be an incredible first lady.

It's his love for Hunter, Ashley, his grandchildren, and the entire Biden family.

And while I first knew Joe as Vice President, I really got to know him as the father who loved Beau, my dear friend, who we remember here today.

To my husband Doug, our children Cole and Ella, my sister Maya, and our whole family—I love you all more than I can express.

We are so grateful to Joe and Jill for welcoming our family into theirs on this incredible journey.

And to the woman most responsible for my presence here today—my mother, Shyamala Gopalan Harris, who is always in our hearts.

When she came here from India at the age of 19, maybe she didn't quite imagine this moment.

But she believed so deeply in an America where a moment like this is possible.

So, I'm thinking about her and about the generations of women—Black women.

Asian, White, Latina, and Native American women throughout our nation's history who have paved the way for this moment tonight.

Women who fought and sacrificed so

much for equality, liberty, and justice for all, including the Black women, who are too often overlooked, but so often prove that they are the backbone of our democracy.

All the women who worked to secure and protect the right to vote for over a century: 100 years ago with the 19th Amendment, 55 years ago with the Voting Rights Act, and now, in 2020, with a new generation of women in our country who cast their ballots and continued the fight for their fundamental right to vote and be heard.

Tonight, I reflect on their struggle, their determination and the strength of their vision—to see what can be unburdened by what has been—I stand on their shoulders.

And what a testament it is to Joe's character that he had the audacity to break one of the most substantial barriers that exists in our country and select a woman as his vice president.

But while I may be the first woman in this

office, I won't be the last.

Because every little girl watching tonight sees that this is a country of possibilities.

And to the children of our country, regardless of your gender, our country has sent you a clear message:

Dream with ambition, lead with conviction, and see yourself in a way that others might not see you, simply because they've never seen it before.

And we will applaud you every step of the way.

To the American people:

No matter who you voted for, I will strive to be the vice president that Joe was to President Obama—loyal, honest, and prepared, waking up every day thinking of you and your families. Because now is when the real work begins.

The hard work. The necessary work. The good work.

The essential work to save lives and beat this pandemic.

To rebuild our economy so it works for working people.

To root out systemic racism in our justice system and society.

To combat the climate crisis.

To unite our country and heal the soul of our nation.

The road ahead will not be easy.

But America is ready. And so are Joe and I.

We have elected a president who represents the best in us.

A leader the world will respect and our children can look up to.

A commander-in-chief who will respect our troops and keep our country safe.

And a president for all Americans.

It is now my great honor to introduce the President-elect of the United States of America, Joe Biden.

Epilogue

On January 6, 2021, the Capitol was attacked by a mob of ultraright supporters of President Trump. They believed that a massive fraud had been perpetrated in the presidential election. It was the day on which Joe Biden was formally recognized by Congress as the next president of the United States.

Right after Mike Pence, vice president of the Trump administration, ritually declared that Joe Biden would be the next president, the Capitol was attacked. Even then, President Trump did not accept the results of the election and insisted that it was a fraud.

At the same time, two new senators were elected in the state of Georgia. They were both Democrats, which meant that the Democratic Party became the majority party in both the House and Senate.

However, there were still many people

frustrated with the results of the presidential and senatorial elections in Georgia. The brutal incursion into the Capitol tells us how badly American society was wounded. It will take time and energy for this injury to heal.

Of course, it is not a good idea to say liberalism is right and conservatism is wrong. What is important is that democracy is maintained. As long as Democrats and Republicans are keeping a sharp eye on each other and exchanging opinions, politics work. And, as long as the balance between the two parties is kept, the country is stable. This how people can manage this complex world.

However, what happened at the beginning of 2021 at the Capitol is nothing but violence. This horrible incident jeopardized democracy itself. This is what caused many Americans to worry, because the peaceful transfer of the power every four years is the pride of American democracy.

That pride was nearly shattered the moment

mobs occupied the building and threw it into confusion. The inauguration ceremony took place with the protection of more than 25,000 National Guards. And President Trump left for Florida without attending the ceremony. It was extraordinary moment in US history.

The task of rebuilding American democracy has just begun. After the inauguration, the team of Joe Biden and Kamala Harris accelerated distribution of COVID-19 vaccine to save American's lives. They also announced the return of the US to the Paris Agreement to mitigate global warming.

The effort to restore a society once divided is not easy. It was Kamala's job to make this long journey successful by supporting Joe Biden.

Keep in mind that this long journey started when George Washington became the first president of the US based on the spirit of the Declaration of Independence. The journey was succeeded by Abraham Lincoln, who abolished slavery. Then, the torch was handed to

President Kennedy, who supported the Civil Right Acts requested by Martin Luther King Jr. and many civil rights activists, including John Lewis. Kamala Harris is now one of the leaders on the democratic path of this great nation.

Word List

A

☐ **abandon** 名①自暴自棄 ②気まま、奔放 動①捨てる、放棄する ②(計画などを)中止する、断念する

☐ **abhor** 動(ひどく)嫌う

☐ **abolish** 動廃止する、撤廃する

☐ **above all** 何よりも

☐ **Abraham Lincoln** エイブラハム・リンカーン《第16代アメリカ合衆国大統領(1861–65)、1809–65》

☐ **abroad** 熟 from abroad 海外から

☐ **abuse** 動虐待する、悪用する 名虐待、悪用、乱用

☐ **accelerate** 動加速する

☐ **accept** 動①受け入れる ②同意する、認める

☐ **according** 副《–to ~》~によれば[よると]

☐ **accordingly** 副①それに応じて、適宜に ②従って、(~と)いうわけだから

☐ **accumulate** 動①蓄積する、積もる ②積み上げる、積み重ねる

☐ **accused** 動 accuse (告訴する)の過去、過去分詞 形告発された、非難された 名《the –》被告人

☐ **achieve** 動成し遂げる、達成する、成功を収める

☐ **acquaint** 動(~を)熟知させる、知り合いにさせる

☐ **acquaintance** 名①知人、知り合い ②面識、知識

☐ **across** 熟 come across ~に出くわす、~に遭遇する

☐ **act** 名行為、行い 動①行動する ②機能する ③演じる

☐ **action** 熟 put one's plan into action 計画を実行に移す woman of action《a –》活動家、行動家

☐ **active** 形①活動的な ②積極的な ③活動[活動]中の

☐ **actively** 副活発に、活動的に

☐ **activist** 名活動家、実践主義者

☐ **activity** 名活動、活気

☐ **actual** 形実際の、現実の

☐ **actually** 副実際に、本当に、実は

☐ **adamantly** 副断固(として)、かたくなに

☐ **add** 動①加える、足す ②足し算をする ③言い添える

☐ **addition** 名①付加、追加、添加 ②足し算 in addition 加えて、さらに

100

□ **adjust** 動①適応する[させる], 慣れる ②調整する ③(意見の食い違い・論争などを)解決する, 調停する ④(間違いなどを)訂正する

□ **administration** 名管理, 統治, 政権

□ **administrative** 形①行政の ②管理の, 運営[経営]上の

□ **adopt** 動①採択する, 選ぶ ②承認する ③養子にする

□ **adopted** 形①養子[養女]になった ②採用された

□ **advantage** 名有利な点[立場], 強み, 優越

□ **affection** 名愛情, 感情

□ **affordable** 形手ごろな[良心的な]価格の

□ **Affordable Care Act** 《The Patient Protection and – 》患者保護ならびに医療費負担適正化法《オバマ元大統領が推進した医療保険制度改革法, 通称オバマケア(Obama Care)》

□ **African** 形アフリカ(人)の 名アフリカ人

□ **after that** その後

□ **age** 熟at the age of ~歳のときに

□ **agency** 名①代理店, 仲介 ②機関, 政府機関 ③媒介, 媒体

□ **agreement** 名①合意, 協定 ②一致

□ **aim** 動①(武器・カメラなどを)向ける ②ねらう, 目指す 名ねらい, 目標

□ **Alameda County** アラメダ郡《カリフォルニア州にある郡。郡庁所在地はオークランド(Oakland)》

□ **all** 熟above all 何よりも all over ~中で, ~の至る所で all over the world 世界中に first of all まず第一に

□ **allow** 動①許す,《 – … to ~》…が~するのを可能にする, …に~させておく ②与える

□ **along with** ~と一緒に

□ **always** 熟not always 必ずしも~であるとは限らない

□ **ambition** 名大望, 野心

□ **amendment** 名①改正, 修正 ②(憲法の)改正案

□ **America** 名アメリカ《国名・大陸》

□ **America First** アメリカ第一主義《孤立主義を強調する米国の外交スタンスを指す言葉, トランプ前大統領が自身のスローガンとした》

□ **American** 形アメリカ(人)の 名アメリカ人

□ **amount** 名①量, 額 ②《the – 》合計 動(総計~に)なる

□ **ancestral** 形祖先の, 先祖代々の

□ **and** 熟and so on ~など, その他もろもろ between A and B AとBの間に both A and B AもBも grow -er and -er ~にますます~する hundreds and thousands of 何百, 何千という more and more ますます

□ **anger** 名怒り 動怒る, ~を怒らせる

□ **announce** 動(人に)知らせる, 公表する

□ **announcement** 名発表, アナウンス, 告示, 声明

□ **another** 熟one another お互い

□ **anti-immigration** 名反移民, 移民排斥 形反移民の, 移民排斥(派)の

□ **anti-Muslim** 名反イスラム教徒 形反イスラム教徒の

□ **apparently** 副見たところ~らしい, 明らかに

□ **appear** 動①現れる, 見えてくる ②(~のように)見える, ~らしい

□ **appearance** 名①現れること, 出現 ②外見, 印象

□ **applaud** 動拍手かっさいする, 賞賛する

□ **apply** 動①申し込む, 志願する ②あてはまる ③適用する

□ **appoint** 動①任命する, 指名する ②（日時・場所などを）指定する

□ **appointment** 名①（会合などの）約束, 予約 ②任命, 指名

□ **appreciate** 動①正しく評価する, よさがわかる ②価値［相場］が上がる ③ありがたく思う

□ **approach** 動①接近する ②話を持ちかける 名接近, （〜へ）近づく道

□ **appropriate** 形①適切な, ふさわしい, 妥当な ②特殊な, 特有の 動①割り当てる ②自分のものにする, 占有する

□ **approved** 動 approve（賛成する）の過去, 過去分詞 形①認可された, 公認の ②定評のある

□ **argue** 動①論じる, 議論する ②主張する

□ **argument** 名①議論, 論争 ②論拠, 理由

□ **Arizona** 名アリゾナ《米国南西部にある州》

□ **arrest** 動逮捕する 名逮捕

□ **arrive in** 〜に着く

□ **as a matter of course** 当然のこと

□ **as a result** その結果（として）

□ **as far as** 〜する限り（では）

□ **as for** 〜に関しては, 〜はどうかと言うと

□ **as long as** 〜する以上は, 〜である限りは

□ **as well** なお, その上, 同様に

□ **as well as** 〜と同様に

□ **Ashley** 名《–Biden》アシュリー・バイデン《ジョー・バイデン（Joe Biden）の娘, 1981–》

□ **Asia** 名アジア

□ **Asian** 名アジア人 形アジアの

□ **aspect** 名①状況, 局面, 側面 ②外観, 様子

□ **assault** 名襲撃, 強襲, 暴行 動襲撃する, 暴行する

□ **assign** 動任命する, 割り当てる 名譲り受け人

□ **assistant** 名助手, 補佐, 店員 形援助の, 補佐の

□ **association** 名①交際, 連合, 結合 ②連想 ③協会, 組合

□ **at issue** 論争中の, （意見が）一致しない

□ **at one time** ある時には, かつては

□ **at that time** その時

□ **at the age of** 〜歳のときに

□ **atmosphere** 名①大気, 空気 ②雰囲気

□ **atrocity** 名①〔戦争時の〕残虐行為 ②残虐さ, 非道さ

□ **attack** 動①襲う, 攻める ②非難する ③（病気が）おかす 名①攻撃, 非難 ②発作, 発病

□ **attempt** 動試みる, 企てる 名試み, 企て, 努力

□ **attend** 動①出席する ②世話をする, 仕える ③伴う ④《–to〜》〜に注意を払う, 専念する, 〜の世話をする

□ **attitude** 名姿勢, 態度, 心構え

□ **attorney** 名弁護士, 法定弁護人

□ **Attorney General** 〈米〉検事総長, 司法長官

□ **audacity** 名①大胆さ, 剛勇 ②厚かましさ, 尊大 ③大胆［尊大］な行為

□ **audience** 名聴衆, 視聴者

□ **authority** 名①権威, 権力, 権限 ②《the -ties》（関係）当局

□ **authorization** 名①権限を与えること, 権威づけ ②許可, 承認, 免許

□ **automatically** 副無意識に, 自動的に, 惰性的に

□ **autonomy** 名①自治（権）, 自治

左側インデックス: A B C D E F G H I J K L M N O P Q R S T U V W X Y Z

国家, 自治体 ②自律(性), 自主(性)

□ **await** 動待つ, 待ち受ける

B

□ **back** 熟come back to ～へ帰って
くる, ～に戻る go back to ～に帰る
[戻る], ～に遡る push back 押し返
す, 押しのける

□ **backbone** 名①背骨 ②主力, 中
心

□ **background** 名背景, 前歴, 生い
立ち

□ **badly** 副①悪く, まずく, へたに
②とても, ひどく

□ **balance** 名①均衡, 平均, 落ち着
き ②てんびん ③残高, 差額 動釣り
合いをとる

□ **ballot** 名①投票用紙 ②投票数
動①投票する ②くじで決める

□ **ban** 名禁止, 禁制 動禁止する

□ **banish** 動追放する, 追い払う

□ **bar** 名①酒場 ②棒, かんぬき ③障
害(物) 動かんぬきで閉める

□ **Barack Obama** バラク・オバ
マ《アメリカ合衆国第44代大統領
(2009-17), 1961-》

□ **barrier** 名さく, 防壁, 障害(物), 障
壁 動防壁で囲む

□ **base** 名基礎, 土台, 本部 動《－on
～》～に基礎を置く, 基づく

□ **based on** 《be－》～に基づく

□ **basically** 副基本的には, 大筋では

□ **basis** 名①土台, 基礎 ②基準, 原理
③根拠 ④主成分 on the basis of ～
に基づいて

□ **Bay Area** 《the－》〔サンフランシ
スコ〕湾岸地帯

□ **bear** 動①運ぶ ②身に着ける ③耐
える ④(子を)産む bear arms 武装
する 名①熊 ②(株取引で)弱気

□ **bearing** 動bear (運ぶ)の現在分

詞 名①態度 ②関係 ③《-s》ベアリ
ング, 軸受け

□ **beat** 動①打つ, 鼓動する ②打ち負
かす 名打つこと, 鼓動, 拍

□ **Beau Biden** ボー・バイデン《ジ
ョー・バイデン (Joe Biden)の長男,
1969-2015》

□ **because of** ～のために, ～の理由
で

□ **beginning** 動begin (始まる)の
現在分詞 名初め, 始まり

□ **behavior** 名振る舞い, 態度, 行動

□ **behind** 前①～の後ろに, ～の背後
に ②～に遅れて, ～に劣って 副①
後ろに, 背後に ②遅れて, 劣って

□ **being** 動be (～である)の現在分
詞 名存在, 生命, 人間 come into
being 生じる, 発生[出現]する
human being 人, 人間

□ **belie** 動〔予想などを〕裏切る, 矛盾
する

□ **believe in** ～を信じる

□ **belong** 動《－to ～》～に属する,
～のものである

□ **belonging** 動belong (属する)の
現在分詞 名《-s》持ち物, 所有物, 財
産

□ **below** 前①～より下に ②～以下
の, ～より劣る 副下に[へ]

□ **benefit** 名①利益, 恩恵 ②(失業
保険・年金などの)手当, 給付(金)
動利益を得る, (～の)ためになる

□ **Berkeley** 名バークレー, バークリ
ー《カリフォルニア州・アラメダ郡の
北部, サンフランシスコ湾の東にある
都市》

□ **Bernie Sanders** バーニー・サ
ンダース《アメリカ合衆国の政治家,
1941-》

□ **better** 熟get better 良くなる, 好
転する

□ **between A and B** AとBの間
に

□ **beyond** 前 ～を越えて，～の向こうに 副 向こうに

□ **bias** 名 偏見，先入見，バイアス 動 偏見をもたせる

□ **Bible** 名 ①《the –》聖書 ②《b-》権威ある書物，バイブル

□ **Biden** 名《Joe –》ジョー・バイデン《アメリカ合衆国第46代大統領 (2021–)，1942–》

□ **bill** 名 ①請求書，勘定書 ②法案 ③紙幣 ④ビラ ⑤くちばし 動 ①請求書を送る ②勘定書に記入する

□ **birthplace** 名 出生地

□ **Black Lives Matter** ブラック・ライヴズ・マター《アフリカ系アメリカ人に対する暴力や人種差別の撤廃を訴える国際的な積極行動主義の運動（スローガン），直訳すると「黒人の命は大切」》

□ **blame** 動 とがめる，非難する 名 ①責任，罪 ②非難

□ **blue-collar** 名 ブルーカラー，肉体労働者 形 ブルーカラーの，肉体労働者の

□ **bold** 形 ①勇敢な，大胆な，奔放な ②ずうずうしい ③派手な ④（文字が）太字の

□ **border** 名 境界，へり，国境 動 ①接する，境をなす ②縁どりをつける

□ **both A and B** AもBも

□ **bound** 動 ①bind（縛る）の過去，過去分詞 ②跳びはねる ③境を接する，制限する 形 ①縛られた，束縛された ②《– for ～》～行きの 名 境界（線），限界

□ **boundary** 名 境界線，限界

□ **braid** 名《ふつう -s》編んだ髪 動 編む，編んで作る

□ **brain** 名 ①脳 ②知力

□ **breathe** 動 ①呼吸する ②ひと息つく，休息する

□ **brilliant** 形 光り輝く，見事な，すばらしい

□ **brink** 名（崖などの）ふち，瀬戸際

□ **brutal** 形 けもののような，残酷な

□ **brutally** 副 残忍に，容赦なく，残酷なまでに，すごく

□ **building** 動 build（建てる）の現在分詞 名 建物，建造物，ビルディング

□ **burden** 名 ①荷 ②重荷 動 荷［負担］を負わす

□ **bus** 動（～を）バスで輸送する

□ **but** 熟 not ～ but … ～ではなくて … nothing but ただ～だけ，～にすぎない

□ **by** 熟 day by day 日ごとに

C

□ **California** 名 カリフォルニア《米国西部，太平洋岸の州》

□ **call for** ～を求める，訴える，～を呼び求める

□ **campaign** 名 ①キャンペーン（活動，運動）②政治運動，選挙運動 ③軍事行動 動 ①従軍する ②運動に参加する

□ **Canada** 名 カナダ《国名》

□ **cancer** 名 がん colon cancer 結腸がん

□ **candidate** 名 ①立候補者 ②学位取得希望者 ③志願者

□ **capital** 名 ①首都 ②大文字 ③資本（金）形 ①首都の ③最も重要な ④大文字の

□ **Capitol** 名《the –》アメリカ合衆国議会議事堂

□ **carbon-dioxide** 名 二酸化炭素，炭酸ガス

□ **career** 名 ①（生涯の・専門的な）職業 ②経歴，キャリア

□ **cast** 動 ①投げる ②役を与える 名 ①投げること ②配役

□ **categorize** 動 分類する，類別する

□ **cause** 熟 root cause 根本的原因

□ **celebrate** 動 ①祝う, 祝福する ②祝典を開く

□ **central** 形 中央の, 主要な

□ **centralized** 形 中央集権化の

□ **ceremony** 名 ①儀式, 式典 ②礼儀, 作法, 形式ばること

□ **certain** 形 ①確実な, 必ず〜する ②(人が)確信した ③ある ④いくらかの 代 (〜の中の)いくつか

□ **challenge** 名 ①挑戦 ②難関 動 挑む, 試す

□ **challenging** 動 challenge (挑戦する)の現在分詞 形 能力が試される, やる気をそそる

□ **champion** 動 擁護する, 支持する

□ **chaos** 名 無秩序, 混乱状態

□ **character** 名 ①特性, 個性 ②(小説・劇などの)登場人物 ③文字, 記号 ④品性, 人格

□ **charge** 動 ①(代金を)請求する ②(〜を…に)負わせる ③命じる 名 ①請求金額, 料金 ②責任 ③非難, 告発

□ **cheerful** 形 上機嫌の, 元気のよい, (人を)気持ちよくさせる

□ **Chennai** 名 チェンナイ《インド東部・ベンガル湾に面するタミル・ナードゥ州の州都》

□ **chief** 名 頭, 長, 親分 形 最高位の, 第一の, 主要な

□ **childhood** 名 幼年[子ども]時代

□ **China** 名 ①中国《国名》②(c-)陶磁器, 瀬戸物

□ **Chinese** 形 中国(人)の 名 ①中国人 ②中国語

□ **choice** 名 選択(の範囲・自由), えり好み, 選ばれた人[物] 形 精選した

□ **chosen as** 《be－》〜として選ばれる

□ **Christian** 名 キリスト教徒, クリスチャン 形 キリスト(教)の

□ **cite** 動 言及する, 引用する 名 言及, 引用

□ **city hall** 〈米〉市庁舎, 市役所

□ **citizen** 名 ①市民, 国民 ②住民, 民間人

□ **civil** 形 ①一般人の, 民間(人)の ②国内の, 国家の ③礼儀正しい

□ **Civil Rights Act** 《the－》公民権法《1964年の公民権法で, 教育・公共の場・雇用における人種差別を禁じた》

□ **Civil Rights Movement** 公民権運動《1950〜60年代にかけて, アメリカの黒人(アフリカ系アメリカ人)が公民権の適用と人種差別の解消を求めて行った大衆運動》

□ **Civil War** 《the－》南北戦争《北部のアメリカ合衆国と南部のアメリカ連合国との間で行われた内戦, 1861–65》

□ **clash** 動 ①(意見, 利害が)衝突する ②(金属同士がぶつかって)ガチャンと鳴る 名 (意見, 利害の)衝突

□ **clear** 形 ①はっきりした, 明白な ②澄んだ ③(よく)晴れた 動 ①はっきりさせる ②片づける ③晴れる 副 ①はっきりと ②すっかり, 完全に

□ **clearly** 副 ①明らかに, はっきりと ②《返答に用いて》そのとおり

□ **climate** 名 気候, 風土, 環境

□ **Clinton** 名 《Hillary－》ヒラリー・クリントン《アメリカ合衆国の政治家, 第42代大統領ビル・クリントンの妻, 1947–》

□ **closely** 副 ①密接に ②念入りに, 詳しく ③ぴったりと

□ **coast** 名 海岸, 沿岸 動 ①滑降する ②(〜の)沿岸を航行する ③楽々とやり遂げる

□ **Cole** 名 《－ Emhoff》コール・エムホフ《カマラ・ハリス (Kamala Harris) の息子, 1995–》

□ **colleague** 名 同僚, 仲間, 同業者

□ **college** 名 団体 electoral college 選挙人団

- [ ] **colon** 名結腸 **colon cancer** 結腸がん
- [ ] **color** 熟 **of color** 有色（人種）の
- [ ] **colorful** 形①カラフルな, 派手な ②生き生きとした
- [ ] **combat** 名戦闘 動戦う, 効果がある
- [ ] **come across** 〜に出くわす, 〜に遭遇する
- [ ] **come back to** 〜へ帰ってくる, 〜に戻る
- [ ] **come into** 〜に入ってくる
- [ ] **come into being** 生じる, 発生［出現］する
- [ ] **come into contact with** 〜と接触する, 〜に出くわす
- [ ] **come into effect** 発効する, 成立する
- [ ] **come to a head** （問題や危険などが）頂点に達する
- [ ] **coming** 動come（来る）の現在分詞 形今度の, 来たるべき 名到来, 来ること
- [ ] **commander-in-chief** 名最高司令官
- [ ] **commit** 動①委託する ②引き受ける ③（罪などを）犯す
- [ ] **commonly** 副一般に, 通例
- [ ] **community** 名①団体, 共同社会, 地域社会 ②《the –》社会（一般）, 世間 ③共有, 共同責任
- [ ] **compare** 動①比較する, 対照する ②たとえる
- [ ] **compared with** 《be –》〜と比較して, 〜に比べれば
- [ ] **competition** 名競争, 競合, コンペ
- [ ] **complain** 動①不平［苦情］を言う, ぶつぶつ言う ②（病状などを）訴える
- [ ] **complaint** 名不平, 不満（の種）
- [ ] **complete** 形完全な, まったくの, 完成した 動完成させる
- [ ] **completely** 副完全に, すっかり
- [ ] **complex** 形入り組んだ, 複雑な, 複合の 名①強迫観念 ②複合体, 複合施設
- [ ] **complexity** 名錯綜, 複雑さ
- [ ] **composed** 動compose（構成する）の過去, 過去分詞 形落ち着いた
- [ ] **compromise** 名妥協, 和解 動譲歩する, 妥協する
- [ ] **concept** 名①概念, 観念, テーマ ②（計画案などの）基本的な方向
- [ ] **concerned** 動concern（関係する）の過去, 過去分詞 形①関係している, 当事者の ②心配そうな, 気にしている
- [ ] **concerning** 動concern（関係する）の現在分詞 前〜についての, 関しての
- [ ] **conclude** 動①終える, 完結する ②結論を下す
- [ ] **condemn** 動①責める ②有罪と判決する
- [ ] **condition** 名①（健康）状態, 境遇 ②《-s》状況, 様子 ③条件 動適応させる, 条件づける
- [ ] **Confederacy** 名《the –》南部連合国（= Confederate States of America）
- [ ] **Confederate States of America** 《the –》南部連合国
- [ ] **conference** 名①会議, 協議, 相談 ②協議会
- [ ] **conflict** 名①不一致, 衝突 ②争い, 対立 ③論争 動衝突する, 矛盾する
- [ ] **confusion** 名混乱（状態）
- [ ] **congress** 名①会議, 大会 ②《C-》（米国などの）国会, 議会 ③協会
- [ ] **congressman** 名〔米国の〕連邦議会議員,〔特に〕下院議員
- [ ] **connected** 動connect（つながる）の過去, 過去分詞 形結合した, 関係のある

□ **consequently** 副したがって, 結果として

□ **conservatism** 名保守主義

□ **conservative** 形①保守的な ②控えめな, 地味な 名〔考えや価値観などが〕保守的な人, 伝統を重んじる人 ②《C-》〔政治的な〕保守系［派〕の人, 保守党支持者

□ **consider** 動①考慮する, ～しようと思う ②(～と)みなす 名気にかける, 思いやる

□ **consist** 動①《- of ～》(部分・要素から)成る ②《- in ～》～に存在する, ～にある

□ **constitution** 名①憲法, 規約 ②構成, 構造

□ **constitutional** 形①憲法の, 合憲の ②体質の

□ **contact** 熟come into contact with ～と接触する, ～に出くわす

□ **contend** 動争う, 競う, 論争する, 強く主張する

□ **continual** 形継続的な, 繰り返される

□ **contract** 名契約(書), 協定 動①契約する ②縮小する

□ **contradiction** 名①否定, 反対 ②矛盾

□ **contrast** 名対照, 対比 動対照させる, よい対象となる

□ **control** 動①管理［支配］する ②抑制する, コントロールする 名①管理, 支配(力) ②抑制

□ **controversy** 名論争, 議論

□ **conventional** 形習慣的な

□ **convey** 動①運ぶ ②伝達する, 伝える ③譲渡する

□ **convict** 動有罪を宣告する 名罪人, 囚人

□ **conviction** 名①信念, 確信 ②有罪(判決)

□ **coordinate** 名①座標 ②調和よく組み合わされたもの, コーディネート 形①(等級・重要度などが)等位の ②座標の 動①調和的になる, 同格になる ②調整する, 協調させる

□ **copy** 名①コピー, 写し ②(書籍の)一部, 冊 ③広告文 動写す, まねる, コピーする

□ **core** 名核心, 中心, 芯 **shaken to the core**《be –》心底まで震える

□ **cost** 名①値段, 費用 ②損失, 犠牲 動(金・費用が)かかる, (～を)要する, (人に金額を)費やさせる

□ **count** 動①数える ②(～を…と)みなす ③重要［大切］である 名計算, 総計, 勘定

□ **counterargument** 名反論

□ **counterattack** 名反撃 動反撃する, 逆襲する

□ **counterfeit** 形偽りの, まがいものの 動偽造する, まねる

□ **countless** 形無数の, 数え切れない

□ **county** 名郡, 州

□ **courage** 名勇気, 度胸

□ **courageous** 形勇気のある

□ **course** 熟**as a matter of course** 当然のこと **of course** もちろん, 当然

□ **court** 名①中庭, コート ②法廷, 裁判所 ③宮廷, 宮殿

□ **courthouse** 名①裁判所 ②〈米〉郡庁舎

□ **cover** 動①覆う, 包む, 隠す ②扱う, (～に)わたる, 及ぶ ③代わりを務める ④補う 名覆い, カバー

□ **COVID-19** 略新型コロナウイルス感染症(= coronavirus disease 2019)

□ **crack** 名①割れ目, ひび ②(裂けるような)鋭い音 動①ひびが入る, ひびを入れる, 割れる, 割る ②鈍い音を出す

□ **create** 動創造する, 生み出す, 引き起こす

□ **creation** 名創造［物］

☐ **creator** 图 創作者, 創造者, 神

☐ **crime** 图 ①(法律上の)罪, 犯罪 ②悪事, よくない行為

☐ **criminal** 形 犯罪の, 罪深い, 恥ずべき 图 犯罪者, 犯人

☐ **crisis** 图 ①危機, 難局 ②重大局面

☐ **critical** 形 ①批評の, 批判的な ②危機的な, 重大な

☐ **critically** 副 ①批判的に(言えば), 酷評して ②非常に, とても, 決定的に

☐ **criticize** 動 ①非難する, あら探しをする ②酷評する ③批評する

☐ **crowd** 動 群がる, 混雑する 图 群集, 雑踏, 多数, 聴衆

☐ **crucial** 形 ①重大な, 決定的な ②致命的な, 正念場で

☐ **cruel** 形 残酷な, 厳しい

☐ **crush** 動 押しつぶす, 砕く, 粉々にする 图 押しつぶすこと

☐ **cultivate** 動 耕す, 栽培する, (才能などを)養う, 育成する

☐ **cultural** 形 文化の, 文化的な

☐ **cure** 图 治療, 治癒, 矯正 動 治療する, 矯正する, 取り除く

☐ **current** 形 現在の, 目下の, 通用[流通]している 图 流れ, 電流, 風潮

☐ **currently** 副 今のところ, 現在

D

☐ **damage** 图 損害, 損傷 動 損害を与える, 損なう

☐ **date** 熟 out of date 時代遅れの

☐ **David Hill** デイヴィッド・ヒル《2004年4月10日, サンフランシスコ市警のアイザック・エスピノザ(Isaac Espinoza)を殺害したギャング》

☐ **day** 熟 day by day 日ごとに every day 毎日 one day (過去の)ある日, (未来の)いつか

☐ **deadly** 形 命にかかわる, 痛烈な, 破壊的な 副 ひどく, 極度に

☐ **death** 图 ①死, 死ぬこと ②《the –》終えん, 消滅 death toll 死亡者数

☐ **debate** 動 ①討論する ②思案する 图 討論, ディベート

☐ **debt** 图 ①借金, 負債 ②恩義, 借り

☐ **decency** 图 上品さ, 礼儀正しさ

☐ **decide to do** ～することに決める

☐ **decided** 動 decide(決定する)の過去, 過去分詞 形 はっきりした, 断固とした

☐ **decision** 图 ①決定, 決心 ②判決

☐ **declaration** 图 ①宣言, 布告 ②告知, 発表

☐ **Declaration of Independence** 《the –》アメリカ独立宣言《1776年7月4日に採択された, 北米13植民地がイギリスから独立したことを宣言する文書》

☐ **declare** 動 ①宣言する ②断言する ③(税関で)申告する

☐ **deeply** 副 深く, 非常に

☐ **default** 图 ①デフォルト, 初期値, 初期設定 ②(義務などの)怠慢, 不履行 ③不参加 動 ①(義務・債務などを)怠る ②デフォルトに設定する

☐ **defeat** 動 ①打ち破る, 負かす ②だめにする 图 ①敗北 ②挫折

☐ **defend** 動 防ぐ, 守る, 弁護する

☐ **defendant** 图 被告(人) 形 被告人の

☐ **defense** 图 ①防御, 守備 ②国防 ③弁護, 弁明

☐ **Delaware** 图 デラウェア《米国東部, 大西洋岸中部に位置する州》

☐ **delegate** 動 派遣する, 委任する, 代表に指名する 图 代表, 代理, 委任

☐ **deliver** 動 ①配達する, 伝える ②達成する, 果たす

☐ **demagogue** 图 扇動政治家, 民衆扇動家

☐ **demand** 動①要求する, 尋ねる ②必要とする 名①要求, 請求 ②需要

☐ **demanding** 形①〔人が〕要求の厳しい, 注文の多い ②〔子どもなどが〕手の掛かる ③〔仕事などが〕多大な努力を要する, 骨の折れる

☐ **democracy** 名民主主義, 民主政治

☐ **democratic** 形①民主主義の, 民主制の ②民主的な ③《D-》〈米〉民主党の

☐ **Democratic Party** 《the –》〈米〉民主党

☐ **demonstration** 名①論証, 証明 ②デモンストレーション, 実演 ③デモ, 示威運動

☐ **denounce** 動非難する, 告発する

☐ **deportation** 名①〔外国人の〕国外退去, 本国送還 ②〔母国からの〕国外追放

☐ **descendant** 名子孫, 末えい, (祖先からの) 伝来物

☐ **desegregation** 名人種差別廃止

☐ **desire** 動強く望む, 欲する 名欲望, 欲求, 願望

☐ **desperate** 形①絶望的な, 見込みのない ②ほしくてたまらない, 必死の

☐ **desperately** 副絶望的に, 必死になって

☐ **destroy** 動破壊する, 絶滅させる, 無効にする

☐ **destruction** 名破壊 (行為・状態)

☐ **detention** 名引き留め, 抑留, 拘留

☐ **determination** 名決心, 決定

☐ **determined** 動determine (決心する) の過去, 過去分詞 形決心した, 決然とした

☐ **devastate** 動荒らす, 荒廃させる, 困惑させる

☐ **develop** 動①発達する [させる]

②開発する

☐ **developing** 動develop (発達する) の現在分詞 形発展 [開発] 途上の

☐ **development** 名①発達, 発展 ②開発

☐ **diagnose** 動診断する

☐ **diametrically** 副正反対に

☐ **dilemma** 名板ばさみ, ジレンマ

☐ **diligent** 形勤勉な, 熱心な, 励んでいる

☐ **diplomacy** 名外交, 外交的手腕

☐ **direct** 形まっすぐな, 直接の, 率直な, 露骨な 副まっすぐに, 直接に 動①指導する, 監督する ②(目・注意・努力などを) 向ける

☐ **direction** 名①方向, 方角 ②《-s》指示, 説明書 ③指導, 指揮

☐ **disappointed** 動disappoint (失望させる) の過去, 過去分詞 形がっかりした, 失望した

☐ **disaster** 名災害, 災難, まったくの失敗

☐ **discriminate** 動①見分ける, 識別する, 区別する ②差別する

☐ **discrimination** 名差別, 区別, 識別

☐ **discuss** 動議論 [検討] する

☐ **disease** 名①病気 ②(社会や精神の) 不健全な状態

☐ **dispute** 名論争, 議論 動反論する, 論争する

☐ **distribution** 名①分配 ②配布, 配給 ③流通 ④分布, 区分

☐ **district** 名①地方, 地域 ②行政区

☐ **distrust** 名不信, 疑惑 動疑う, 不信感を抱く

☐ **diverse** 形①種々の, 多様な ②異なった

☐ **diversity** 名多様性, 相違

☐ **divide** 動分かれる, 分ける, 割れる, 割る

☐ **division** 名①分割 ②部門 ③境界

A
B
C
D
E
F
G
H
I
J
K
L
M
N
O
P
Q
R
S
T
U
V
W
X
Y
Z

④割り算

☐ **divorce** 動離婚する 名離婚, 分離

☐ **document** 名文書, 記録 動(～を)記録する

☐ **domination** 名支配, 統治, 優位

☐ **Donald J. Harris** ドナルド・J・ハリス《カマラ・ハリス (Kamala Harris) の父, 1938–》

☐ **Donald Trump** ドナルド・トランプ《アメリカ合衆国第45代大統領 (2017–21), 1946–》

☐ **doubt** 名①疑い, 不確かなこと ②未解決点, 困難 **there is no doubt that**〔that以下〕ということは疑いようがない 動疑う

☐ **Doug Emhoff** ダグ・エムホフ《カマラ・ハリス (Kamala Harris) の夫, 1964–》

☐ **down** 熟 **settle down** 落ち着く, 定住する

☐ **DREAM Act** ドリーム法《非正規移民の子どもたちの米国滞在・教育を保護する法案》

☐ **driver** 名①運転手 ②(馬車の) 御者

☐ **drop out of** ～からこぼれ落ちる, ～から手を引く

☐ **drug** 名薬, 麻薬, 麻酔薬

☐ **due** 形予定された, 期日のきている, 支払われるべき **due to** ～によって, ～が原因で 名当然の権利 **due process** (法の) 適正手続き

☐ **duty** 名①義務 (感), 責任 ②職務, 任務, 関税

☐ **dynamic** 形活動的な, 動的な, ダイナミックな

E

☐ **each other** お互いに

☐ **ease** 名安心, 気楽 動安心させる, 楽にする, ゆるめる

☐ **eastern** 形①東方の, 東向きの ②東洋の, 東洋風の

☐ **economic** 形経済学の, 経済上の

☐ **economically** 副経済的に, 節約して

☐ **economist** 名①経済学者 ②倹約家

☐ **economy** 名①経済, 財政 ②節約

☐ **educated** 動 educate (教育する) の過去, 過去分詞 形教養のある, 教育を受けた

☐ **education** 名教育, 教養

☐ **effect** 名①影響, 効果, 結果 ②実施, 発効 **come into effect** 発効する, 成立する **in effect** 有効な, 事実上 動もたらす, 達成する

☐ **effort** 名努力 (の成果)

☐ **elect** 動選ぶ, (～することに) 決める, 選挙する 形選ばれた

☐ **election** 名選挙, 投票

☐ **elector** 名①有権者, 選挙人 ②〈米〉大統領選挙人

☐ **electoral** 形選挙の **electoral college** 選挙人団

☐ **elementary** 形①初歩の ②単純な, 簡単な

☐ **Ella** 名《– Emhoff》エラ・エムホフ《カマラ・ハリス (Kamala Harris) の娘, 1999–》

☐ **emblematic** 形象徴の

☐ **emission** 名放出, 放射, 発射, 発光, 排気

☐ **emotion** 名感激, 感動, 感情

☐ **emotional** 形①感情の, 心理的な ②感情的な, 感激しやすい

☐ **emphasize** 動①強調する ②重視する

☐ **encourage** 動①勇気づける ②促進する, 助長する

☐ **encouragement** 名激励, 励み, 促進

☐ **endorse** 動①(小切手などに) 裏

書する ②是認する

□ **endowed** 形①寄付を受けた, 寄贈された ②〔才能などを〕授かった, 生まれながらに持っている ③〔責任などを〕負わされた

□ **enemy** 名敵

□ **energetic** 形エネルギッシュな, 精力的な, 活動的な

□ **enforce** 動（法律などを）実行する, 実施する, 施行する

□ **enforcement** 名〔法律などの〕施行, 実施, 執行

□ **England** 名①イングランド ②英国

□ **enough to do** ～するのに十分な

□ **enrich** 動豊かにする, 充実させる

□ **ensuing** 形その後の［に続く・に起こった］

□ **entertainment** 名①楽しみ, 娯楽 ②もてなし, 歓待

□ **entire** 形全体の, 完全な, まったくの

□ **entirety** 名①完全である［欠けるものがない］こと ②《the － 》〔量や程度などの〕全部, 全体

□ **environment** 名①環境 ②周囲（の状況）, 情勢

□ **environmental** 形①環境の, 周囲の ②環境保護の

□ **epilogue** 名①（劇の）納め口上, エピローグ ②終章, 終節

□ **episode** 名①挿話, 出来事 ②（テレビ番組の）1回放映分 ③（シリーズ物の）第～話

□ **equal** 形等しい, 均等な, 平等な 動匹敵する, 等しい 名同等のもの［人］

□ **equality** 名平等, 等しいこと

□ **equally** 副等しく, 平等に

□ **era** 名時代, 年代

□ **erupt** 動（火山が）噴火する, 噴出する, 爆発する, （戦争が）勃発する

□ **escape** 動逃げる, 免れる, もれる 名逃亡, 脱出, もれ

□ **Espinoza** 名《Isaac － 》アイザック・エスピノザ《サンフランシスコ市警察官, 2004年4月10日に地元ギャングのデイヴィッド・ヒル（David Hill）に殺害された》

□ **essential** 形本質的な, 必須の 名本質, 要点, 必需品

□ **establish** 動確立する, 立証する, 設置［設立］する

□ **ethnic** 形民族の, 人種的な, エスニックな 名民族の一員, 人種的少数派

□ **Europe** 名ヨーロッパ

□ **European** 名ヨーロッパ人 形ヨーロッパ（人）の

□ **evaluate** 動①価値をはかる ②評価する, 査定する

□ **even if** たとえ～でも

□ **even then** その時でさえ

□ **even though** ～であるけれども, ～にもかかわらず

□ **eventually** 副結局は

□ **ever more** これまで以上に

□ **every day** 毎日

□ **everybody** 代誰でも, 皆

□ **everyone** 代誰でも, 皆

□ **evidence** 名①証拠, 証人 ②形跡

□ **exam** 名《略式》テスト, 試験

□ **example** 熟 for example たとえば

□ **except** 前～を除いて, ～のほかは except for ～を除いて, ～がなければ 接～ということを除いて

□ **exception** 名例外, 除外, 異論

□ **exclude** 動①排除する, 除く ②（～の）余地を与えない, 考慮しない

□ **exclusive** 形排他的な, 独占的な

□ **execute** 動①実行する, 執行する ②死刑にする

□ **executive** 形実行の, 執行の

111

名①高官, 実行委員 ②重役, 役員, 幹部

□ **exercise** 名①運動, 体操 ②練習 動①運動する, 練習する ②影響を及ぼす

□ **exist** 動存在する, 生存する, ある, いる

□ **existent** 形現存の, 存在する

□ **expect** 動予期[予測]する, (当然のこととして)期待する

□ **expense** 名①出費, 費用 ②犠牲, 代価

□ **experiment** 名実験, 試み 動実験する, 試みる

□ **experimental** 形実験の, 試験的な

□ **express** 動表現する, 述べる 形①明白な ②急行の

□ **expression** 名①表現, 表示, 表情 ②言い回し, 語句

□ **extraordinary** 形異常な, 並はずれた, 驚くべき

□ **extreme** 形極端な, 極度の, いちばん端の 名極端

F

□ **face** 熟in (the) face of ~の面前で, ~に直面して

□ **fact** 熟in fact つまり, 実は, 要するに

□ **fail** 動①失敗する, 落第する[させる] ②《- to ~》~し損なう, ~できない ③失望させる 名失敗, 落第点

□ **fairly** 副①公平に ②かなり, 相当に

□ **fake** 動見せかける, でっち上げる, だます, 偽造する 名にせもの 形にせの

□ **familiar** 形①親しい, 親密な ②《be - with ~》~に精通している, ~と親しい ③普通の, いつもの, おなじみの

□ **famous for** 《be -》~で有名である

□ **fanatical** 形熱狂[狂信]的な

□ **far** 熟as far as ~する限り(では)

□ **fate** 名①《時にF-》運命, 宿命 ②破滅, 悲運 動(~の)運命にある

□ **fear** 名①恐れ ②心配, 不安 動①恐れる ②心配する

□ **fearful** 形①恐ろしい ②心配な, 気づかって

□ **fearsome** 形恐ろしい, ものすごい

□ **federal** 形連邦政府の, 連邦の

□ **feeling** 動feel (感じる)の現在分詞 名①感じ, 気持ち ②触感, 知覚 ③同情, 思いやり, 感受性 形感じる, 感じやすい, 情け深い

□ **female** 形女性の, 婦人の, 雌の 名婦人, 雌

□ **figure** 名①人[物]の姿, 形 ②図(形) ③数字 動①描写する, 想像する ②計算する ③目立つ, (~として)現れる

□ **final** 形最後の, 決定的な 名①最後のもの ②期末[最終]試験 ③《-s》決勝戦

□ **finance** 名①財政, 財務 ②《銀行からの》資金, 融資 ③《-s》財政状態, 財源 動資金を融通する

□ **financial** 形①財務(上)の, 金融(上)の ②金融関係者の

□ **finding** 動find (見つける)の現在分詞 名①発見 ②《-s》発見物, 調査結果 ③《-s》認定, 決定, 答申

□ **finished** 動finish (終わる)の過去, 過去分詞 形①終わった, 仕上がった ②洗練された ③もうだめになった

□ **firm** 名会社, 事務所 形堅い, しっかりした, 断固とした 副しっかりと

□ **first of all** まず第一に

□ **Florida** 名フロリダ《米国南東部・メキシコ湾と大西洋に挟まれるフロ

リダ半島の全域を占める州》

- [ ] **flow** 動流れ出る, 流れる, あふれる 名①流出 ②流ちょう(なこと)

- [ ] **Floyd** 名《George –》ジョージ・フロイド《2020年5月25日, ミネソタ州ミネアポリスで逮捕される最中に警官に死亡させられたアフリカ系アメリカ人》

- [ ] **foot** 熟on foot 歩いて

- [ ] **for example** たとえば

- [ ] **for ~ years** ~年間, ~年にわたって

- [ ] **force** 名力, 勢い 動①強制する, 力ずくで~する, 余儀なく~させる ②押しやる, 押し込む

- [ ] **foreclosure** 名《法律》〔抵当物, 担保物件の〕請け戻し権喪失, 担保権執行, フォークロージャー

- [ ] **foreign-born** 形外国生まれの 名《the –》外国生まれの人々

- [ ] **forest fire** 森林火災, 山火事

- [ ] **forestland** 名森林地

- [ ] **form** 名①形, 形式 ②書式 動形づくる

- [ ] **formal** 形正式の, 公式の, 形式的な, 格式ばった

- [ ] **formally** 副①正式に, 公式に ②形式的に ③儀式ばって, 堅苦しく

- [ ] **former** 形①前の, 先の, 以前の ②《the –》(二者のうち)前者の

- [ ] **fortunately** 副幸運にも

- [ ] **fragmented** 形崩壊した, 分裂した

- [ ] **frame** 名骨組み, 構造, 額縁 動形づくる, 組み立てる

- [ ] **fraud** 名詐欺, 詐欺師

- [ ] **freedom** 名①自由 ②束縛がないこと

- [ ] **frequently** 副頻繁に, しばしば

- [ ] **friendship** 名友人であること, 友情

- [ ] **front** 熟in front of ~の前に, ~の正面に

- [ ] **frustrated** 動frustrate (挫折させる)の過去・過去分詞 形挫折した, 失望した

- [ ] **frustration** 名欲求不満, 失意, 挫折

- [ ] **fund** 名①資金, 基金, 財源 ②金 ③公債, 国債 動①資金を出す ②長期公債の借り換えをする

- [ ] **fundamental** 名基本, 原理 形基本の, 根本的な, 重要な

- [ ] **funeral** 名葬式, 葬列 形葬式の

G

- [ ] **gain** 動①得る, 増す ②進歩する, 進む 名①増加, 進歩 ②利益, 得ること, 獲得

- [ ] **gang** 名①群れ, 一団 ②ギャング, 暴力団 ③(子ども, 若者の)遊び仲間, 非行少年グループ

- [ ] **gas** 名①ガス, 気体 ②ガソリン 動ガス[ガソリン]を供給する

- [ ] **gather** 動①集まる, 集める ②生じる, 増す ③推測する

- [ ] **gender** 名(社会的に決められた)性, 性別

- [ ] **gene** 名遺伝子

- [ ] **general** 形①全体の, 一般の, 普通の ②おおよその ③(職位の)高い, 上級の in general 一般に, たいてい 名大将, 将軍

- [ ] **generally** 副①一般に, だいたい ②たいてい

- [ ] **generation** 名①同世代の人々 ②一世代 ③発生, 生成

- [ ] **generosity** 名①寛大, 気前のよさ ②豊富さ

- [ ] **George Floyd** ジョージ・フロイド《2020年5月25日, ミネソタ州ミネアポリスで逮捕される最中に警官に死亡させられたアフリカ系アメリカ人》

113

- [ ] **George Washington** ジョージ・ワシントン《アメリカ合衆国初代大統領（1789–97），1732–99》
- [ ] **Georgia** 名 ジョージア《米国の南東部にある州》
- [ ] **get better** 良くなる，好転する
- [ ] **get out of** 〜から下車する，〜から外へ出る［抜け出る］
- [ ] **get to know** 知るようになる，知り合う
- [ ] **global** 形 地球（上）の，地球規模の，世界的な，国際的な **global warming** 地球温暖化
- [ ] **globally** 副 グローバルに，地球規模で（は）
- [ ] **globe** 名 ①球 ②地球
- [ ] **go back to** 〜に帰る［戻る］，〜に遡る
- [ ] **goddess** 名 女神
- [ ] **goods** 名 ①商品，品物 ②財産，所有物
- [ ] **gotten** 動 get（得る）の過去分詞
- [ ] **government** 名 政治，政府，支配
- [ ] **governor** 名 ①知事 ②支配者，（学校・病院・官庁などの）長
- [ ] **graduate** 動 卒業する 名 卒業生，（〜学校の）出身者
- [ ] **grandchildren** 名 grandchild（孫）の複数
- [ ] **grant** 動 ①許可する，承認する ②授与する，譲渡する ③（なるほどと）認める 名 授与されたもの
- [ ] **granted** 熟 take 〜 for granted 〜を当然のことと思う
- [ ] **grateful** 形 感謝する，ありがたく思う
- [ ] **gratitude** 名 感謝（の気持ち），報恩の念
- [ ] **greenhouse** 名 温室
- [ ] **Gretchen Whitmer** グレッチェン・ホイットマー《アメリカ合衆国・第49代ミシガン州知事（2019–），

1971–》
- [ ] **grief** 名 （深い）悲しみ，悲嘆
- [ ] **grievance** 名 ①（労働条件に対する）不平 ②憤り
- [ ] **grow -er and -er** 〜にますます〜する
- [ ] **grow up** 成長する，大人になる
- [ ] **growing** 動 grow（成長する）の現在分詞 形 成長期にある，大きくなりつつある
- [ ] **guarantee** 名 保証，保証書，保証人 動 保証する，請け合う
- [ ] **guard** 名 ①警戒，見張り ②番人 動 番をする，監視する，守る
- [ ] **guilty** 形 有罪の，やましい
- [ ] **gun** 名 銃，大砲 動 銃で撃つ **gun control** 銃規制

H

- [ ] **half-solved** 形 半分解決された，中途半端な
- [ ] **hall** 名 公会堂，ホール，大広間，玄関
- [ ] **hand** 熟 on the other hand 一方，他方では
- [ ] **handling** 動 handle（手を触れる）の現在分詞 名 ①取り扱い，処理 ②（サッカーなどでの）ハンド
- [ ] **happiness** 名 幸せ，喜び
- [ ] **hard** 熟 try hard to 〜に尽力する **work hard to do** 〜するために懸命に働く
- [ ] **harsh** 形 厳しい，とげとげしい，不快な
- [ ] **harshly** 副 ①厳しく，過酷に，荒々しく ②目障りなほどに，ギラギラして
- [ ] **hate** 動 嫌う，憎む，（〜するのを）いやがる 名 憎しみ
- [ ] **heal** 動 癒える，癒す，治る，治す
- [ ] **healer** 名 治療する人，薬

114

□ **healing** 動heal (いえる)の現在分詞 形治療の, 病気を治す, いやす 名治療

□ **hearing** 動hear (聞く)の現在分詞 名①聞くこと, 聴取, 聴力 ②聴聞会, ヒアリング

□ **heartless** 形無情な, 残酷な

□ **heat** 名①熱, 暑さ ②熱気, 熱意, 激情 動熱する, 暖める

□ **heatedly** 副熱くなって, 興奮して, 激しく

□ **hesitate** 動ためらう, ちゅうちょする

□ **hidden** 動hide (隠れる)の過去分詞 形隠れた, 秘密の **hidden ball trick** 〈野球〉隠し球

□ **hide** 動隠れる, 隠す, 隠れて見えない, 秘密にする

□ **highly** 副①大いに, 非常に ②高度に, 高位に ③高く評価して, 高価で

□ **Hillary Clinton** ヒラリー・クリントン《アメリカ合衆国の政治家, 第42代大統領ビル・クリントンの妻, 1947–》

□ **Hindu** 名ヒンドゥー 形ヒンドゥー教の, ヒンドゥー文化の, (北部)インドの

□ **Hindu-dominant** 形ヒンドゥー教徒が多い[主流の]

□ **historical** 形歴史の, 歴史上の, 史実に基づく

□ **hold out** 〔希望を〕抱かせる

□ **homeland** 名母国, 祖国, 本土

□ **homeowner** 名住宅[自宅]所有者

□ **honest** 形①正直な, 誠実な, 心からの ②公正な, 感心な

□ **Hong Kong** 香港《中華人民共和国の特別行政区》

□ **honor** 名①名誉, 光栄, 信用 ②節操, 自尊心 動尊敬する, 栄誉を与える

□ **horrible** 形恐ろしい, ひどい

□ **how to** ～する方法

□ **Howard University** ハワード大学《米国ワシントンD.C.にある私立大学, カマラ・ハリス (Kamala Harris) の母校》

□ **however** 副たとえ～でも 接けれども, だが

□ **human being** 人, 人間

□ **hundreds and thousands of** 何百, 何千という

□ **Hunter** 名《– Biden》ハンター・バイデン《ジョー・バイデン (Joe Biden) の次男, 1970–》

I

□ **I can't breathe** 「息ができない」《ブラック・ライヴズ・マター運動と関連して警察の暴力行為への抗議を示すスローガン。白人警官によって逮捕中に窒息死した2人のアフリカ系アメリカ人男性, エリック・ガーナー (2014) とジョージ・フロイド (2020) が発した言葉から派生》

□ **iconic** 形象徴的な

□ **identify** 動①(本人・同一と) 確認する, 見分ける ②意気投合する

□ **identity** 名①同一であること ②本人であること ③独自性

□ **ideology** 名観念, イデオロギー

□ **if** 熟even if たとえ～でも **see if** ～かどうかを確かめる **wonder if** ～ではないかと思う

□ **ignite** 名点火 動火がつく[つける], 発火する

□ **ignore** 動無視する, 怠る

□ **illegal** 形違法な, 不法な

□ **imagine** 動想像する, 心に思い描く

□ **immediate** 形さっそくの, 即座の, 直接の

115

□ **immediately** 副すぐに, ～するやいなや

□ **immense** 形巨大な, 計り知れない, すばらしい

□ **immigrant** 名移民, 移住者 形移民に関する

□ **immigration** 名①移民局, 入国管理 ②移住, 入植

□ **import** 動輸入する 名輸入, 輸入品

□ **import tariff** 輸入関税

□ **importantly** 副重大に, もったいぶって

□ **imposing** 動impose (課す)の現在分詞 形印象的な, 人目をひく, 立派な

□ **imprisonment** 名投獄, 交流

□ **in (the) face of** ～の面前で, ～に直面して

□ **in addition** 加えて, さらに

□ **in effect** 有効な, 事実上

□ **in fact** つまり, 実は, 要するに

□ **in front of** ～の前に, ～の正面に

□ **in general** 一般に, たいてい

□ **in order to** ～するために, ～しようと

□ **in other words** すなわち, 言い換えれば

□ **in public** 人前で, 公然と

□ **in record numbers** 記録的な数で

□ **in the middle of** ～の真ん中[中ほど]に

□ **in the name of** ～の名において, ～という名目で

□ **in the way of** ～の邪魔になって, 行く手を塞いで

□ **in time** 間に合って, やがて

□ **in-person** 形〔人が〕直接会う, 生で出演する

□ **inauguration** 名就任式, 就任演説

□ **incident** 名出来事, 事故, 事変, 紛争 形①起こりがちな ②付随する

□ **include** 動含む, 勘定に入れる

□ **including** 動include (含む)の現在分詞 前～を含めて, 込みで

□ **inclusive** 形包括的な, 勘定に入れた

□ **income** 名収入, 所得, 収益

□ **increase** 動増加[増強]する, 増やす, 増える 名増加(量), 増大

□ **incredible** 形①信じられない, 信用できない ②すばらしい, とてつもない

□ **incumbent** 形現職の, 在職の

□ **incursion** 名侵略, 襲撃, 侵入

□ **indeed** 副①実際, 本当に ②《強意》まったく 間本当に, まさか

□ **independence** 名独立心, 自立

□ **independent** 形独立した, 自立した

□ **India** 名インド《国名》

□ **Indian** 名①インド人 ②(アメリカ)インディアン 形①インド(人)の ②(アメリカ)インディアンの

□ **indiscriminately** 副見境なく, 無差別に

□ **individual** 形独立した, 個性的な, 個々の 名個体, 個人

□ **industrial** 形工業の, 産業の

□ **industry** 名産業, 工業

□ **influence** 名影響, 勢力 動影響をおよぼす

□ **influential** 形影響力の大きい, 有力な

□ **infringement** 名〔法律・契約の〕違反, 〔権利の〕侵害

□ **inherit** 動相続する, 受け継ぐ

□ **inherited** 形遺伝の[による], 生まれつきの, 系統を引く

□ **inhuman** 形人間味のない, 冷酷

な

□ **initiate** 動〔計画・事業・話し合いなどを〕始める，開始する

□ **injury** 名①けが ②侮辱，無礼

□ **injustice** 名不当，不正（行為）

□ **innocent** 名無邪気な人，罪のない人 形無邪気な，無実の

□ **insignia** 名①〔ある集団の一員であることを表す〕記章，バッジ ②〔他と区別するための〕しるし，記号

□ **insist** 動①主張する，断言する ②要求する

□ **instantly** 副すぐに，即座に

□ **instead** 副その代わりに **instead of** ～の代わりに，～をしないで

□ **insurance** 名保険

□ **integrate** 動①統合する，一体化する ②溶け込ませる，溶け込む，差別をなくす

□ **integrity** 名完全性，高潔

□ **intense** 形①強烈な，激しい ②感情的な

□ **intentionally** 副故意に

□ **interest** 熟 show an interest in ～に興味を示す，～に関心を見せる

□ **interesting** 動 interest（興味を起こさせる）の現在分詞 形おもしろい，興味を起こさせる

□ **interestingly** 副面白い[興味深い]ことに

□ **internal** 形内部の，国内の，本質的な 名内部

□ **intervene** 動①間に入る，介入する，干渉する ②仲裁する，調停する

□ **intervention** 名介入，仲裁，調停，干渉

□ **intolerance** 名①不寛容，狭量 ②耐えられないこと

□ **invisible** 名目に見えないもの 形目に見えない，表に出ない

□ **involved** 動 involve（含む）の過去，過去分詞 形①巻き込まれている，関連する ②入り組んだ，込み入っている

□ **ironically** 副皮肉にも，皮肉なことに

□ **Isaac Espinoza** アイザック・エスピノザ《サンフランシスコ市警察官，2004年4月10日に地元ギャングのデイヴィッド・ヒル（David Hill）に殺害された》

□ **issue** 名①問題，論点 ②発行物 ③出口，流出 **at issue** 論争中の，（意見が）一致しない 動①（～から）出る，生じる ②発行する

□ **It is ～ for someone to ...** （人）が…するのは～だ

□ **itself** 代それ自体，それ自身

J

□ **jail** 名刑務所 動拘置する，投獄する

□ **Jamaica** 名ジャマイカ《国名》

□ **Jamaican** 形ジャマイカ（人）の

□ **Japanese** 形日本（人・語）の 名①日本人 ②日本語

□ **jeopardize** 動危うくする，脅かす，台無しにする

□ **Jill** 名《– Biden》ジル・バイデン《ジョー・バイデン（Joe Biden）の妻でファーストレディ，1951-》

□ **Joe Biden** ジョー・バイデン《アメリカ合衆国第46代大統領（2021-），1942-》

□ **John Kelly** ジョン・ケリー《アメリカ合衆国の政治家，トランプ政権で国土安全保障長官・大統領首席補佐官を務めた，1950-》

□ **John Lewis** ジョン・ルイス《アメリカ合衆国の政治家・公民権運動活動家，1940-2020》

□ **journalist** 名報道関係者，ジャーナリスト

□ **journey** 名①（遠い目的地への）

旅 ②行程

☐ **joy** 图喜び, 楽しみ

☐ **judge** 動判決を下す, 裁く, 判断する, 評価する 图裁判官, 判事, 審査員

☐ **judicial** 形裁判(官)の, 司法の

☐ **justice** 图①公平, 公正, 正当, 正義 ②司法, 裁判(官)

☐ **juvenile** 形児童の, 少年[少女]の

☐ **Juvenile Court** 少年裁判所

K

☐ **Kamala Harris** カマラ・ハリス《アメリカ合衆国第49代副大統領(2021-), 1964-》

☐ **Kennedy** 图《John F. -》ジョン・F・ケネディ《アメリカ合衆国第35代大統領(1961-63), 1917-63》

☐ **kidnap** 動誘拐する 图誘拐

☐ **knelt** 動kneel(ひざまずく)の過去, 過去分詞

☐ **know** 熟get to know 知るようになる, 知り合う

☐ **knowledge** 图知識, 理解, 学問

☐ **known as** 《be -》～として知られている

L

☐ **lack** 動不足している, 欠けている 图不足, 欠乏

☐ **Lakshmi** 图〔ヒンドゥー教の〕ラクシュミー神《富や豊穣の女神》

☐ **largely** 副大いに, 主として

☐ **Latina** 图ラテン系の女性, 〈米〉ラテンアメリカ系女性住民

☐ **law enforcement** 法の執行

☐ **lawyer** 图弁護士, 法律家

☐ **leadership** 图指揮, リーダーシップ

☐ **lean** 動①もたれる, 寄りかかる ②傾く, 傾ける 形やせた, 不毛の

☐ **leave for** ～に向かって出発する

☐ **led** 動lead(導く)の過去, 過去分詞

☐ **left-wing** 形左派(寄り)の, 左翼の

☐ **legacy** 图遺産, 遺贈品

☐ **legal** 形法律(上)の, 正当な

☐ **legally** 副合法的に, 法律的に

☐ **less** 形～より小さい[少ない] 副～より少なく, ～ほどでなく

☐ **level** 图①水平, 平面 ②水準 形①水平の, 平たい ②同等[同位]の 動①水平にする ②平等にする

☐ **liberal** 形①自由主義の, 進歩的な ②気前のよい 图自由主義者

☐ **liberalism** 图①〔政治上の〕進歩主義, 改革主義 ②〔政治上の〕自由主義, リベラリズム ③自由市場経済理論 ④《キリスト教》〔プロテスタントの〕自由主義運動

☐ **liberty** 图①自由, 解放 ②《-ties》特権, 特典 ③《-ties》勝手な振る舞い

☐ **lie** 動①うそをつく ②横たわる, 寝る ③(ある状態に)ある, 存在する 图うそ, 詐欺

☐ **life** 熟way of life 生き様, 生き方, 暮らし方

☐ **lifestyle** 图生活様式, ライフスタイル

☐ **lifetime** 图①一生, 生涯 ②寿命

☐ **like this** このような, こんなふうに

☐ **likely** 形①ありそうな, (～)しそうな ②適当な 副たぶん, おそらく

☐ **limited** 動limit(制限する)の過去, 過去分詞 形限られた, 限定の

☐ **Lincoln** 图《Abraham -》エイブラハム・リンカーン《第16代アメリカ合衆国大統領(1861-65), 1809-65》

☐ **living** 動live(住む)の現在分詞 图生計, 生活 形①生きている, 現存の ②使用されている ③そっくりの

□ **locate** 動 置く, 居住する［させる］

□ **logical** 形 論理学の, 論理的な

□ **long** 熟 **as long as** 〜する以上は, 〜である限りは

□ **look** 熟 **look up to** 〜を仰ぎ見る **take a look at** 〜をちょっと見る

□ **loss** 名 ①損失（額・物）, 損害, 浪費 ②失敗, 敗北

□ **lotus** 名 ハス（蓮）《植物》

□ **low-income** 形 低所得の

□ **loyal** 形 忠実な, 誠実な 名 忠実, 愛国者

M

□ **mail-in** 形 郵送の

□ **main** 形 主な, 主要な

□ **mainly** 副 主に

□ **maintain** 動 ①維持する ②養う

□ **major** 形 ①大きいほうの, 主な, 一流の ②年長［古参］の 名 ①陸軍少佐 ②専攻科目 動 専攻する

□ **majority** 名 ①大多数, 大部分 ②過半数

□ **make a speech** 演説をする

□ **make it** やり遂げる

□ **make sure** 確かめる, 確認する

□ **make up** 作り出す, 〜を構成［形成］する

□ **making** 動 make（作る）の現在分詞 名 制作, 製造

□ **male** 形 男の, 雄の 名 男, 雄

□ **male-oriented** 形 男性志向の, 男性向けの, 男性優位の

□ **manage** 動 ①動かす, うまく処理する ②経営［管理］する, 支配する ③どうにか〜する

□ **mandate** 名 命令

□ **manipulate** 動 操る, 操作する, 巧みに扱う

□ **marked** 動 mark（印をつける）の過去, 過去分詞 形 ①目立つ, 顕著な ②印のある, マークされた

□ **marriage** 名 ①結婚（生活・式）②結合, 融合, （吸収）合併

□ **married** 動 marry（結婚する）の過去, 過去分詞 形 結婚した, 既婚の

□ **Martin Luther King Jr.** マーティン・ルーサー・キング・ジュニア, キング牧師《アフリカ系アメリカ人公民権運動の指導者として活動した, 1929–68》

□ **mask** 名 面, マスク 動 マスクをつける

□ **massive** 形 ①巨大な, 大量の ②堂々とした

□ **mate** 名 仲間, 連れ 動 ①交尾する［させる］②仲間になる, 結婚する

□ **maternal** 形 ①母親の, 母親らしい ②母方の

□ **matter** 熟 **as a matter of course** 当然のこと **matter of〈a–〉**〜の問題 **no matter** 〜を問わず

□ **Maya** 《– Harris》マヤ・ハリス《カマラ・ハリス（Kamala Harris）の妹, 1967–》

□ **McGill University** マギル大学《カナダ・ケベック州のモントリオールに本部を置く公立大学》

□ **means of** 〜する手段

□ **mechanism** 名 機構, 仕組み

□ **media** 名 メディア, マスコミ, 媒体

□ **medical** 形 ①医学の ②内科の 名 健康診断, 身体検査

□ **memoir** 名 ［個人の］回想［回顧］録, 体験記,《-s》自伝

□ **mend** 動 直す, 繕う, よくなる 名 修理, 修繕

□ **mention** 動（〜について）述べる, 言及する 名 言及, 陳述

□ **mercy** 名 ①情け, 哀れみ, 慈悲 ②ありがたいこと, 幸運

□ **Mexican** 形 メキシコ（人）の 名 メキシコ人

□ **Mexico** 名 メキシコ《国名》

□ **Michigan** 名 ミシガン《米国中西

119

部に位置する州》

- ☐ **middle** 图中間, 最中 **in the middle of** ～の真ん中［中ほど］に 圏中間の, 中央の

- ☐ **might** 動《may の過去》①～かも しれない ②～してもよい, ～できる 图力, 権力

- ☐ **migrant** 图渡り鳥, 移住者, 季節 労働者

- ☐ **Mike Pence** マイク・ペンス《ア メリカ合衆国の政治家, トランプ政 権時の第48代副大統領（2017-21）, 1959-》

- ☐ **mile** 图①マイル《長さの単位。 1,609m》②〈-s〉かなりの距離

- ☐ **milestone** 图①道しるべ, マイル 標石, 一里塚 ②〔歴史・人生・計画な どにおける〕画期的事件, 節目

- ☐ **military** 圏軍隊［軍人］の, 軍事の 图〈the –〉軍, 軍部

- ☐ **militia** 图市民軍, 民兵（組織）

- ☐ **Milwaukee** 图ミルウォーキー 《ウィスコンシン州最大の都市》

- ☐ **mind** 图①心, 精神, 考え ②知性 動①気にする, いやがる ②気をつけ る, 用心する

- ☐ **Minneapolis** 图ミネアポリス《ミ ネソタ州最大の都市》

- ☐ **minority** 图少数派, 少数民族

- ☐ **mitigate** 動和らげる, 軽減する

- ☐ **mix** 動①混ざる, 混ぜる ②（～を） 一緒にする 图混合（物）

- ☐ **mixed** 動 mix（混ざる）の過去, 過 去分詞 圏①混合の, 混ざった ②男 女共学の

- ☐ **mob** 图群集, やじ馬 動群がる, 襲 う, 殺到する

- ☐ **moderate** 圏穏やかな, 適度な, 手ごろな 動穏やかにする, 抑える

- ☐ **modern** 圏現代［近代］の, 現代的 な, 最近の 图現代［近代］人

- ☐ **Momala** 略モマラ（= mother Kamala）《カマラ・ハリス（Kamala

Harris）の継子からの呼称》

- ☐ **moment** 图①瞬間, ちょっとの間 ②（特定の）時, 時期

- ☐ **momentous** 圏重大な, 由々しき

- ☐ **momentum** 图勢い, 弾み, 推進 力, 運動量

- ☐ **Montreal** 图モントリオール《カ ナダ・ケベック州の都市》

- ☐ **more** 熟 ever more これまで以上 に **and more and more** ますます **more than** ～以上

- ☐ **moreover** 副その上, さらに

- ☐ **mortgage** 图抵当（権）動抵当に 入れる

- ☐ **mount** 動（程度, 圧力などが）高ま る, 上昇する

- ☐ **movement** 图①動き, 運動 ② 〈-s〉行動 ③引っ越し ④変動

- ☐ **multitudinous** 圏非常に多くの, 多様な

- ☐ **murder** 图人殺し, 殺害, 殺人事件 動殺す

- ☐ **Muslim** 图イスラム教徒, ムスリ ム 圏イスラム教［文明］の

- ☐ **mutual** 圏相互の, 共通の

- ☐ **mythological** 圏神話の

N

- ☐ **name** 熟 in the name of ～の名に おいて, ～という名目で

- ☐ **narcotic** 图①麻酔薬, 睡眠薬 ② 麻薬（中毒者）, 薬物 ③〔退屈で〕眠く なる（ような）もの 圏①麻薬の, 麻 酔効果のある ②麻薬中毒者（用）の ③〔退屈で〕眠くなる（ような）

- ☐ **nation** 图国, 国家,《the –》国民

- ☐ **national** 圏国家［国民］の, 全国の

- ☐ **National Convention of the Democratic Party** 民主党全国 大会《4年に1度, 民主党が正副大統領

の指名候補の選出時に開く大会》

☐ **national health insurance**
国民健康保険

☐ **nationwide** 形全国的な 副全国
的に, 全国では

☐ **native** 形①出生(地)の, 自国の
②(〜に)固有の, 生まれつきの, 天然
の 名(ある土地に)生まれた人

☐ **nearly** 副①近くに, 親しく ②ほ
とんど, あやうく

☐ **necessary** 形必要な, 必然の 名
《-s》必要品, 必需品

☐ **need to do** 〜する必要がある

☐ **needy** 形貧乏な, お金に困って, す
がるような

☐ **negative** 形①否定的な, 消極的
な ②負の, マイナスの, (写真が)ネ
ガの 名①否定, 反対 ②ネガ, 陰画,
負数, マイナス

☐ **neglect** 動①無視する, 怠る ②放
置する, 軽視する 名無視, 軽視, 怠慢

☐ **negotiator** 名ネゴシエーター,
交渉人, 協議者

☐ **neighborhood** 名近所(の人々),
付近

☐ **Nevada** 名ネバダ《米国西部に位
置する州》

☐ **nevertheless** 副それにもかかわ
らず, それでもやはり

☐ **newcomer** 名新しく来た人, 初
心者

☐ **news** 名報道, ニュース, 便り, 知
らせ

☐ **no matter** 〜を問わず

☐ **nobody** 代誰も[1人も]〜ない

☐ **nominate** 動①指名する, 推薦す
る ②指定する

☐ **nomination** 名指名, 任命, 推薦

☐ **norm** 名基準, 規範

☐ **not always** 必ずしも〜であると
は限らない

☐ **not quite** まったく〜だというわ

けではない

☐ **not 〜 but …** 〜ではなくて…

☐ **nothing but** ただ〜だけ, 〜にす
ぎない

☐ **notion** 名観念, 概念, 意志

☐ **notorious** 形(悪いことで)有名な,
名うての

☐ **number** 熟in record numbers
記録的な数で the number of 〜の
数

O

☐ **Oakland** 名オークランド《カリフ
ォルニア州・アラメダ郡の郡庁所在
地》

☐ **Obama** 名《Barack –》バラク・オ
バマ《アメリカ合衆国第44代大統領
(2009–17), 1961–》

☐ **Obama Care** オバマケア《オバ
マ元大統領が推進した医療保険制
度改革法, 正式名称は The Patient
Protection and Affordable Care Act》

☐ **obsess** 動支配する, つきまとう,
頭から離れない obsess over 〜に執
着する

☐ **obstacle** 名障害(物), じゃま(な
物)

☐ **occupy** 動①占領する, 保有する
②居住する ③占める ④(職に)つく,
従事する

☐ **occur** 動(事が)起こる, 生じる, (考
えなどが)浮かぶ

☐ **of color** 有色(人種)の

☐ **of course** もちろん, 当然

☐ **offender** 名違反者, 犯罪者

☐ **officer** 名役人, 公務員, 警察官

☐ **on foot** 歩いて

☐ **on one's own** 自力で

☐ **on the basis of** 〜に基づいて

☐ **on the other hand** 一方, 他方
では

□ **on the point of** 今にも～しそうで

□ **one** 熟 **at one time** ある時には, かつては **on one's own** 自力で **one another** お互い **one day** (過去の) ある日, (未来の) いつか **one of ～** の1つ [人] **put one's plan into action** 計画を実行に移す

□ **onward** 副 前方へ, 進んで 形 前方への

□ **openly** 副 率直に, 公然と

□ **opponent** 形 敵対する, 反対する 名 競争相手, 敵, 反対者

□ **opportunity** 名 好機, 適当な時期 [状況]

□ **oppose** 動 反対する, 敵対する

□ **opposite** 形 反対の, 向こう側の 前 ～の向こう側に 名 反対の人 [物]

□ **opposition** 名 ①反対 ②野党

□ **oppress** 動 圧迫する, 苦しめる

□ **oppression** 名 圧迫, 抑圧, 重荷

□ **order** 熟 **in order to ～** するために, ～しようと

□ **ordinary** 形 ①普通の, 通常の ②並の, 平凡な

□ **Oregon** 名 オレゴン《米国西海岸に位置する州》

□ **organized** 動 organize (組織する) の過去, 過去分詞 形 組織化された, よくまとまった

□ **origin** 名 起源, 出自

□ **original** 形 ①始めの, 元の, 本来の ②独創的な 名 原型, 原文

□ **originally** 副 ①元は, 元来 ②独創的に

□ **other** 熟 **each other** お互いに **in other words** すなわち, 言い換えれば **on the other hand** 一方, 他方では

□ **out of date** 時代遅れの

□ **outline** 名 ①外形, 輪郭 ②概略

□ **outrageous** 形 怒り狂った, 極悪な, 乱暴な, とんでもない

□ **ovation** 名 盛大な拍手, オベーション **standing ovation** 総立ちの拍手喝采

□ **over** 熟 **all over ～** 中で, ～の至る所で **all over the world** 世界中に

□ **overcome** 動 勝つ, 打ち勝つ, 克服する

□ **overlook** ①見落とす, (チャンスなどを) 逃す ②見渡す ③大目に見る 名 見晴らし

□ **overnight** 副 一晩中, 夜通し 名 一泊旅行 形 ①夜通しの ②一泊の

□ **owe** 動 ①(～を) 負う, (～を人の) お陰とする ②(金を) 借りている, (人に対して～の) 義務がある

□ **own** 熟 **on one's own** 自力で

□ **owner** 名 持ち主, オーナー

P

□ **Painganadu Gopalan** パインガナドゥ・ゴーパーラン《カマラ・ハリス (Kamala Harris) の祖父, 1911–98》

□ **palpable** 形 明白な

□ **pandemic** 名 パンデミック《複数の国や全世界など, 広域でまん延する深刻な感染病の大流行》

□ **parent** 名 《-s》両親

□ **Paris Agreement** 《the –》パリ協定《2015年12月12日に採択された, 気候変動抑制に関する多国間の国際的な協定》

□ **parole** 名 〈仏語〉仮出所, 仮釈放, 執行猶予

□ **part** 熟 **take part in ～** に参加する

□ **participate** 動 参加する, 加わる

□ **particularly** 副 特に, とりわけ

□ **partly** 副 一部分は, ある程度は

□ **partner** 名 配偶者, 仲間, 同僚 動 (～と) 組む, 提携する

□ **pass away** 亡くなる, 死ぬ

□ **passing** 動 pass（過ぎる）の現在分詞 形 通り過ぎる, 一時的な 名 ①通行, 通過 ②合格, 及第

□ **passionate** 形 情熱的な, (感情が)激しい, 短気な

□ **past** 形 過去の, この前の 名 過去(の出来事) 前《時間・場所》～を過ぎて, ～を越して 副 通り越して, 過ぎて

□ **path** 名 ①（踏まれてできた）小道, 歩道 ②進路, 通路

□ **patrol** 動 ①巡回, パトロール ②巡回者, 偵察隊 動 巡回する, パトロールする

□ **pave** 動 舗装する　**pave the way** 道を開く

□ **pay** 動 ①支払う, 払う, 報いる, 償う ②割に合う, ペイする 名 給料, 報い

□ **peaceful** 形 平和な, 穏やかな

□ **penalty** 名 刑罰, 罰, ペナルティー

□ **pendulum** 名 振り子, 行ったり来たりするもの

□ **penetrate** 動 ①貫く, 浸透する ②見抜く

□ **Pennsylvania** 名 ペンシルベニア《米国北東部, 大西洋岸中部に位置する州》

□ **performance** 名 ①実行, 行為 ②成績, できばえ, 業績 ③演劇, 演奏, 見世物

□ **period** 名 ①期, 期間, 時代 ②ピリオド, 終わり

□ **permanent** 形 永続する, 永久の, 長持ちする

□ **permit** 動 ①許可する ②(物・事が)可能にする 名 許可(証), 免許

□ **perpetrate** 動 ①〔犯罪などを〕実行する ②〔不都合なことを〕やらかす, しでかす

□ **persistent** 形 ①しつこい, 頑固な ②持続する, 永続的な

□ **personal** 形 ①個人の, 私的な ②本人自らの

□ **PhD** 略 博士号, 博士課程 (= Doctor of Philosophy)

□ **phenomenon** 名 ①現象, 事象 ②並はずれたもの [人]

□ **philosopher** 名 哲学者, 賢者

□ **philosophy** 名 哲学, 主義, 信条, 人生観

□ **photograph** 名 写真 動 写真を撮る

□ **pioneer** 名 開拓者, 先駆者

□ **place** 熟 **take place** 行われる, 起こる

□ **plan** 熟 **put one's plan into action** 計画を実行に移す

□ **pleased** 動 please（喜ばす）の過去, 過去分詞 形 喜んだ, 気に入った

□ **pledge** 名 ①誓約, 約束 ②担保 動 誓約する [させる], 誓う, 保障する

□ **plus** 前 ～を加えて 形 ①正の, プラスの ②有利な ②上の部の 名 ①正符号, プラス, 正数 ②利点, 付加物 副 その上に, さらに

□ **point** 熟 **on the point of** 今にも～しそうで　**point of view** 考え方, 視点　**point out** 指し示す, 目を向けさせる

□ **pointed** 動 point（指す）の過去, 過去分詞 形 先のとがった, 鋭い

□ **police officer** 警察官

□ **policeman** 名 警察官

□ **policy** 名 ①政策, 方針, 手段 ②保険証券

□ **political** 形 ①政治の, 政党の ②策略的な

□ **politician** 名 政治家, 政略家

□ **politics** 名 政治(学), 政策

□ **poll** 名 ①投票(数),《the -s》投票場 ②世論調査 動 （票を）得る, 投票する

□ **population** 名 人口, 住民(数)

□ **position** 名 ①位置, 場所, 姿勢 ②地位, 身分, 職 ③立場, 状況　**put**

123

oneself in the position 自分を～の立場に置く　動置く，配置する

□ **possess** 動①持つ，所有する　②（心などを）保つ，制御する

□ **possessed** 動 possess (持つ) の過去，過去分詞　形取りつかれた

□ **possession** 名①所有 (物)　②財産，領土

□ **possibility** 名可能性，見込み，将来性

□ **possible** 形①可能な　②ありうる，起こりうる

□ **poverty** 名貧乏，貧困，欠乏，不足

□ **prefer** 動 (～のほうを) 好む，(～のほうが) よいと思う

□ **prejudice** 名偏見，先入観

□ **prepared** 形準備 [用意] のできた

□ **presence** 名①存在すること　②出席，態度

□ **present** 熟 up to the present 現在に至るまで

□ **presentation** 名①提出，提示　②実演，プレゼンテーション

□ **presidency** 名大統領の任務 [任期]

□ **president** 名①大統領　②社長，学長，頭取

□ **president-elect** 名〈米〉〔就任前の〕次期大統領〈米〉大統領に選ばれた，次期大統領の [となる]

□ **presidential** 形大統領の

□ **presidential election** 大統領選挙

□ **press** 動①圧する，押す，プレスする　②強要する，迫る　名①圧迫，押し，切迫　②出版物 [社]，新聞

□ **pressure** 名プレッシャー，圧力，圧縮，重荷　動圧力をかける

□ **pride** 名誇り，自慢，自尊心　動《～oneself》誇る，自慢する

□ **priority** 名優先 (すること)，優先度 [順位]

□ **prison** 名①刑務所，監獄　②監禁
　prison sentence 実刑判決

□ **private** 形①私的な，個人の　②民間の，私立の　③内密の，人里離れた

□ **privilege** 名①特権，特典，格別の光栄　②(基本的) 人権

□ **Pro-Trump** 形トランプ (前大統領) 支持の

□ **proactive** 形〔行動などが〕先を見越した，積極的な，前向きな

□ **proceeding** 名①手順，手続き，進行　②《法律》訴訟 (手続き)

□ **process** 名①過程，経過，進行　②手順，方法，製法，加工

□ **product** 名①製品，産物　②成果，結果

□ **productive** 形生産的な，豊富な

□ **professional** 形専門の，プロの，職業的な　名専門家，プロ

□ **professor** 名教授，師匠

□ **profit** 名利益，利潤，ため　動利益になる，(人の) ためになる，役立つ

□ **progress** 名①進歩，前進　②成り行き，経過　動前進する，上達する

□ **progressive** 形進歩的な，前進する　名革新主義者

□ **promote** 動促進する，昇進 [昇級] させる

□ **promotion** 名①昇進　②促進　③宣伝販売

□ **prompt** 形迅速な，機敏な　動促す，鼓舞する，促して～させる

□ **proper** 形①適した，適切な，正しい　②固有の

□ **properly** 副適切に，きっちりと

□ **property** 名①財産，所有物 [地]　②性質，属性

□ **proportion** 名①割合，比率，分け前　②釣り合い，比例

□ **proposal** 名①提案，計画　②プロポーズ

□ **prosecute** 動起訴する，告訴する，

遂行する

□ **prosecutor** 名 ①検察官 ②訴追者

□ **protection** 名 保護, 保護するもの［人］

□ **protest** 動 ①主張［断言］する ②抗議する, 反対する 名 抗議（書）, 不服

□ **protester** 名 〔個人または集団で〕抗議（行動）をする人, デモに参加する人

□ **prove** 動 ①証明する ②（～であることが）わかる, (～と)なる

□ **provided** 動 provide（供給する）の過去, 過去分詞 接 もし～ならば, 仮に～とすれば

□ **public** 名 一般の人々, 大衆 形 公の, 公開の in public 人前で, 公然と

□ **punishment** 名 ①罰, 処罰 ②罰を受けること

□ **pursue** 動 ①追う, つきまとう ②追求する, 従事する

□ **pursuit** 名 追跡, 追求

□ **push back** 押し返す, 押しのける

□ **put one's plan into action** 計画を実行に移す

□ **put oneself in the position** 自分を～の立場に置く

Q

□ **quality** 名 ①質, 性質, 品質 ②特性 ③良質

□ **quandary** 名 板挟み, 困惑, 窮地

□ **quit** 動 やめる, 辞職する, 中止する

□ **quite** 熟 not quite まったく～だというわけではない

□ **quotation** 名 ①引用, 引用文［句］②相場, 時価 ③見積もり

□ **quote** 動 ①引用する ②（価格などを）見積もる 名 ①引用（句）②見積もり

R

□ **racial** 形 人種の, 民族の

□ **racism** 名 人種差別（主義）

□ **radical** 形 急進的な, 過激な 名 急進主義者, 過激派

□ **radically** 副 徹底的に, 急進的に, 過激に, 元来

□ **raise** 動 ①上げる, 高める ②起こす ③～を育てる ④（資金を）調達する 名 高める［上げる］こと, 昇給

□ **rape** 名 レイプ, 性的暴行

□ **rapidly** 副 速く, 急速, すばやく, 迅速に

□ **rate** 名 ①割合, 率 ②相場, 料金 動 ①見積もる, 評価する［きんゐる］②等級をつける

□ **rather** 副 ①むしろ, かえって ②かなり, いくぶん, やや ③それどころか逆に rather than ～よりもしろ

□ **re-elect** 動 〔～を〕再選する

□ **ready to** 《be－》すぐに［いつでも］～できる, ～する構えで

□ **reality** 名 現実, 実在, 真実(性)

□ **realize** 動 理解する, 実現する

□ **reasoning** 名 ①論法, 推理, 論理的思考 ②論拠, 根拠

□ **rebuild** 動 再建する, 改造する

□ **rebuilding** 名 再建, 復元, 改築, 立て直し

□ **recently** 副 近ごろ, 最近

□ **recession** 名 景気後退, 不況, 後退

□ **reclaim** 動 ①返還を要求する, 再要求する, 取り戻す ②埋め立てる, 再生利用する

□ **recognize** 動 認める, 認識［承認］する

□ **record** 名 ①記録, 登録, 履歴 ②（音楽などの）レコード in record numbers 記録的な数で 動 ①記録［登録］する ②録音［録画］する

□ **recover** 動 ①取り戻す, ばん回す

る ②回復する

□ **rectify** 動〔誤りなどを〕正す，修正する，〔違反などを〕是正する

□ **reduce** 動①減じる ②しいて～させる，(～の) 状態にする

□ **refer** 動①〔～に〕言及する，触れる ②〔～を〕引用する ③〔～を〕参照する，照会する

□ **reflect** 動映る，反響する，反射する

□ **reform** 動改善する，改革する 名改善，改良

□ **refuse** 動拒絶する，断る 名くず，廃物

□ **regain** 動取り戻す，(～に) 戻る

□ **regardless** 形無頓着な，注意しない 副それにもかかわらず，それでも

□ **region** 名①地方，地域 ②範囲

□ **registered** 動 register (登録する) の過去，過去分詞 **registered by**《be – 》～によって示される 形登録された

□ **rejoice** 動喜ぶ

□ **related** 動 relate (関係がある) の過去，過去分詞 形①関係のある，関連した ②姻戚の

□ **relation** 名①(利害) 関係，間柄 ②親戚

□ **relationship** 名関係，関連，血縁関係

□ **release** 動①解き放す，釈放する ②免除する ③発表する，リリースする 名解放，釈放

□ **relief** 名 (苦痛・心配などの) 除去，軽減，安心，気晴らし

□ **relieved** 形安心した，ほっとした

□ **religion** 名宗教，～教，信条

□ **religious** 形①宗教の ②信心深い

□ **reluctant** 形気乗りしない，しぶしぶの

□ **remain** 動①残っている，残る ②(～の) ままである〔いる〕 名《-s》①

残り (もの) ②遺跡

□ **remedy** 名治療 (薬)，改善 (案) 動治療する，(状況を) 改善する

□ **renovate** 動①修理〔改装・復元〕する，新しくする ②〔元気を〕回復する ③刷新する，革新する

□ **repeatedly** 副繰り返して，たびたび

□ **represent** 動①表現する ②意味する ③代表する

□ **representative** 名①代表 (者)，代理人 ②代議士 ③典型，見本 形①代表の，代理の ②典型的な

□ **Republican** 形《米》共和党の 名《米》共和党員

□ **Republican Party**《the – 》《米》共和党

□ **request** 名願い，要求 (物)，需要 動求める，申し込む

□ **research** 名調査，研究 動調査する，研究する

□ **resident** 名居住者，在住者

□ **resilience** 名①弾性，復元力 ②回復力，立ち直る力

□ **resist** 動抵抗〔反抗・反撃〕する，耐える

□ **resistance** 名抵抗，反抗，敵対

□ **resource** 名①資源，財産 ②手段，方策

□ **respect** 名①尊敬，尊重 ②注意，考慮 動尊敬〔尊重〕する

□ **responsible** 形責任のある，信頼できる，確実な

□ **restore** 動元に戻す，復活させる

□ **restrict** 動制限する，禁止する

□ **result** 名結果，成り行き，成績 **as a result** その結果 (として) 動 (結果として) 起こる，生じる，結局～になる

□ **retain** 動①保つ，持ち続ける ②覚えている

□ **return to** ～に戻る，～に帰る

□ **review** 图①書評, 評論 ②再調査 ③復習 動①批評する ②再調査する ③復習する

□ **revitalize** 動〔～に〕新しい活力を 与える, 〔～を〕復興させる, 再生する

□ **rid** 動取り除く

□ **rifle** 图ライフル銃

□ **rig** 動〔価格・取引・入札・選挙などを〕 不正操作する

□ **right-wing** 形右派の, 右翼の

□ **ring** 图①輪, 円形, 指輪 ②競技場, リング 動①輪で取り囲む ②鳴る, 鳴らす ③電話をかける

□ **risk** 图危険 動危険にさらす, 賭け る, 危険をおかす

□ **ritually** 副儀式上, 儀式として

□ **rival** 图競争相手, 匹敵する人 動競 争する

□ **role** 图①(劇などの)役 ②役割, 任 務

□ **root** 图①根, 根元 ②根源, 原因 ③ 《-s》先祖, ルーツ **root cause** 根本的 原因 動根づかせる, 根づく

□ **run in** ～に出場する, ～に出馬させ る

□ **running** 動run (走る)の現在分詞 图ランニング, 競走 形①走ってい る ②上演中の ③連続する

□ **running mate** 〈米〉〔共同候補で ある〕副大統領[知事]候補

□ **rural** 形田舎の, 地方の

S

□ **sacrifice** 動〔～に〕生け贄をささ げる, 〔～のために〕犠牲になる

□ **sale** 图販売, 取引, 大売り出し

□ **salvation** 图救出, 救済, 救い

□ **same** 熟**the same ～ as** [**that**] ……と同じ(ような)～

□ **San Francisco** サンフランシス コ《カリフォルニア州北部に位置する 都市》

□ **Sanders** 图《Bernie – 》バーニー・ サンダース《アメリカ合衆国の政治家, 1941–》

□ **scale** 图①目盛り ②規模, 割合, 程 度, スケール ③うろこ(鱗) ④てん びん, はかり 動はかりにかける, は かる

□ **scapegoat** 图身代わり, 贖罪のヤ ギ

□ **scar** 图傷跡

□ **scheme** 图計画, スキーム, たくら み, 仕組み, 枠組み 動たくらむ

□ **schooler** 图生徒

□ **search** 動捜し求める, 調べる 图 捜査, 探索, 調査

□ **sector** 图①(産業などの)部門, セ クター ②(幾何で)扇形

□ **secure** 形①安全な ②しっかりし た, 保証された 動①安全にする ② 確保する, 手に入れる

□ **security** 图①安全(性), 安心 ② 担保, 抵当,《-ties》有価証券

□ **seduce** 動誘惑する, そそのかす, くどく

□ **see if** ～かどうかを確かめる

□ **see oneself in a way** 自分を ～な視点から見る

□ **seek** 動捜し求める, 求める

□ **seem** 動(～に)見える, (～のよう に)思われる

□ **seen as** 《be – 》～として見られる

□ **segregate** 動分離する, 隔離する

□ **segregation** 图分離, 隔離, 人種 差別

□ **select** 動選択する, 選ぶ 形選んだ, 一流の, えり抜きの

□ **self-evident** 形自明の(理であ る), 分かりきった

□ **senate** 图①《the S-》(米・仏などの) 上院 ②《the – 》(古代ローマの)元老

院 ③（大学などの）評議会

□ **senator** 图 上院議員, 元老院議員, （大学の）評議員

□ **senatorial** 形 上院（議員）の［から成る］

□ **sense** 图 ①感覚, 感じ ②《-s》意識, 正気, 本性 ③常識, 分別, センス ④意味 動 感じる, 気づく

□ **sensitive** 形 敏感な, 感度がいい, 繊細な

□ **sentence** 图 ①文 ②判決, 宣告 **prison sentence** 実刑判決 動 判決を下す, 宣告する

□ **sentiment** 图 気持ち, 感情, 感傷

□ **separate** 動 ①分ける, 分かれる, 隔てる ②別れる, 別れさせる 形 分かれた, 別れた, 別々の

□ **September 11 attacks** 9.11テロ事件, 9月11日同時多発テロ《2001年9月11日にニューヨークなどで起こった同時多発テロ, ハイジャックされた旅客機が世界貿易センタービルに激突・崩壊した》

□ **serious** 形 ①まじめな, 真剣な ②重大な, 深刻な,（病気などが）重い

□ **seriously** 副 ①真剣に, まじめに ②重大に

□ **seriousness** 图 まじめ, 真剣, 深刻

□ **serve** 動 ①仕える, 奉仕する ②（客の）応対をする, 給仕する, 食事［飲み物］を出す ③（役目を）果たす, 務める, 役に立つ ④（球技で）サーブをする

□ **set off** 区別する, 仕切る

□ **setting** 動 set（置く）の現在分詞 图 設定, 周囲の環境

□ **settle down** 落ち着く, 定住する

□ **settled** 動 settle（安定する）の過去, 過去分詞 形 固定した, 落ち着いた, 解決した

□ **settlement** 图 ①定住, 入植地, 集落 ②合意, 解決, 清算

□ **settler** 图 移住者, 入植者

□ **severely** 副 厳しく, 簡素に

□ **sex** 图 性, 性別, 男女

□ **sexual** 形 性の, 性的な, セクシャルな

□ **shaken** 動 shake（振る）の過去分詞 **shaken to the core**《be-》心底まで震える

□ **sharp** 形 ①鋭い, とがった ②刺すような, きつい ③鋭敏な ④急な 副 ①鋭く, 急に ②（時間が）ちょうど

□ **shatter** 動 打ち砕く, 損なう, こなごなになる

□ **shift** 動 移す, 変える, 転嫁する 图 ①変化, 移動 ②交替,（交代制の）勤務（時間）, シフト

□ **shocked** 形 ～にショックを受けて, 憤慨して

□ **shocking** 動 shock（ショックを与える）の現在分詞 形 衝撃的な, ショッキングな

□ **shoulder** 图 肩 動 肩にかつぐ, 肩で押し分けて進む

□ **show an interest in** ～に興味を示す, ～に関心を見せる

□ **Shyamala Gopalan Harris** シャーマラ・ゴーパーラン・ハリス《カマラ・ハリス（Kamala Harris）の母, 1938-2009》

□ **side** 图 側, 横, そば, 斜面 形 ①側面の, 横の ②副次的な 動 （～の）側につく, 賛成する

□ **similar** 形 同じような, 類似した, 相似の

□ **similarly** 副 同様に, 類似して, 同じように

□ **simply** 副 ①簡単に ②単に, ただ ③まったく, 完全に

□ **simultaneously** 副 同時に, 一斉に

□ **situation** 图 ①場所, 位置 ②状況, 境遇, 立場

□ **skillful** 形 熟練した, 腕のいい

□ **skinny** 形 骨と皮ばかりの，やせた

□ **slave** 名 奴隷 動 (奴隷のように) あくせく働く

□ **slavery** 名 奴隷制度，奴隷状態

□ **slightly** 副 わずかに，いささか

□ **smart** 形 ①利口な，抜け目のない ②きちんとした，洗練された ③激しい，ずきずきする 動 ひりひり[ずきずき]痛む

□ **SNS** 略 ソーシャルネットワーキングサービス (= social networking service)

□ **so** 熟 and so on ～など，その他もろもろ so that ～するために，それで，～できるように so ～ that … 非常に～なので…

□ **so-called** 形 いわゆる

□ **social** 形 ①社会の，社会的な ②社交的な，愛想のよい

□ **society** 名 社会，世間

□ **soldier** 名 兵士，兵卒

□ **solution** 名 ①分解，溶解 ②解決，解明，回答

□ **something** 代 ①ある物，何か ②いくぶん，多少

□ **sometimes** 副 時々，時たま

□ **sorrow** 名 悲しみ，後悔

□ **soul** 名 ①魂 ②精神，心

□ **source** 名 源，原因，もと

□ **South Eastern Asia** 東南アジア

□ **southern** 形 南の，南向きの，南からの

□ **Southern States** 《the –》南部諸州《南北戦争時に奴隷制存続を主張して，アメリカ合衆国を脱退・アメリカ連合国を結成した南部11州のこと》

□ **southernmost** 形 最南端の

□ **speaking** 動 speak (話す) の現在分詞 形 話す，ものを言う 名 話すこと，談話，演説

□ **speculate** 動 ①思索する，推測する ②投機する

□ **speech** 熟 make a speech 演説をする

□ **spirit** 名 ①霊 ②精神，気力

□ **split** 動 裂く，裂ける，割る，割れる，分裂させる[する] 名 ①裂くこと，割れること ②裂け目，割れ目

□ **stable** 形 安定した，堅固な，分解しにくい 名 馬小屋，厩舎

□ **staff** 名 職員，スタッフ 動 配置する

□ **stage** 名 ①舞台 ②段階 動 上演する

□ **stake** 名 ①棒，くい ②賭け金 動 ①賭ける ②くいで囲む

□ **stance** 名 心構え，姿勢，立場

□ **stand in the way** 邪魔 [妨げ] になる

□ **stand against** ～に反対する立場をとる

□ **stand for** ～を意味する，～を支持する

□ **stand up** 立ち上がる

□ **standing ovation** 総立ちの拍手喝采

□ **stark** 形 ①[場所などが] 荒涼とした ②全くの

□ **start doing** ～し始める

□ **start to do** ～し始める

□ **state** 名 ①あり様，状態 ②国家，(アメリカなどの) 州 ③階層，地位 動 述べる，表明する

□ **statement** 名 声明，述べること

□ **statistics** 名 統計 (学)，統計資料

□ **status** 名 ①(社会的な) 地位，身分，立場 ②状態

□ **steady** 形 ①しっかりした，安定した，落ち着いた ②堅実な，まじめな

□ **stepmother** 名 義母，継母

□ **stimulate** 動 ①刺激する ②促す，活性化させる ③元気づける

□ **stoutly** 副 ①強く, 頑丈に ②〔態度などが〕断固として, 毅然と

□ **strained** 形〔事態・雰囲気・人間関係などが〕張り詰めた, 緊迫した

□ **strategist** 名戦略を立てる人, 戦略家

□ **strategy** 名戦略, 作戦, 方針

□ **strength** 名①力, 体力 ②長所, 強み ③強度, 濃度

□ **strident** 形執拗な, 耳障りな, 大げさな

□ **strive** 動努める, 奮闘する

□ **stroller** 名①放浪者 ②折りたたみ式の乳母車

□ **strongly** 副強く, 頑丈に, 猛烈に, 熱心に

□ **struggle** 動もがく, 奮闘する 名もがき, 奮闘

□ **substantial** 形実体の, 本質的な, 実質上の

□ **succeed** 動①成功する ②(〜の)跡を継ぐ

□ **successful** 形成功した, うまくいった

□ **such a** そのような

□ **such as** たとえば〜, 〜のような

□ **such 〜 as ...** …のような〜

□ **suffer** 動①(苦痛・損害などを)受ける, こうむる ②(病気に)なる, 苦しむ, 悩む

□ **suffering** 動suffer (受ける)の現在分詞 名苦痛, 苦しみ, 苦難

□ **suffocation** 名息の根を止めること, 窒息させること

□ **sunshine** 名日光

□ **super** 形超一流の, 特大の

□ **superior** 形優れた, 優秀な, 上方の 名優れた人, 目上(の人)

□ **Superior Court** 《the - 》〔米国の特定の州における〕上位裁判所

□ **support** 動①支える, 支持する ②養う, 援助する 名①支え, 支持 ②援助, 扶養

□ **supporter** 名後援者, 支持者, サポーター, 支柱

□ **supremacist** 名至上主義者

□ **Supreme Court** 《the - 》〔国や連邦・州の〕最高裁判所

□ **Supreme Court Judge** 最高裁判所判事

□ **sure** 熟make sure 確かめる, 確認する

□ **surprised** 動surprise (驚かす)の過去, 過去分詞 形驚いた

□ **survive** 動①生き残る, 存続する, なんとかなる ②長生きする, 切り抜ける

□ **suspect** 動疑う, (〜ではないかと)思う 名容疑者, 注意人物

□ **suspicion** 名①容疑, 疑い ②感づくこと

□ **suspicious** 形あやしい, 疑い深い

□ **sustain** 動持ちこたえる, 持続する, 維持する, 養う

□ **swing** 動①揺り動かす, 揺れる ②回転する, ぐるっと回す 名①揺れ, 振ること, 振動 ②ぶらんこ

□ **swing state** 〈米〉選挙結果を左右する州《大統領選挙において, 選挙結果が共和党と民主党の候補者間で「揺れる州」または「激戦州」のこと》

□ **sworn** 動swear (誓う)の過去分詞

□ **swung** 動swing (回転する)の過去, 過去分詞

□ **symbol** 名シンボル, 象徴

□ **symbolize** 動①記号を用いる ②象徴する, 象徴とみなす

□ **sympathy** 名①同情, 思いやり, お悔やみ ②共鳴, 同感

□ **synergy** 名シナジー, 相乗効果〔作用〕

□ **systemic** 形体系の, システムの

130

T

- [ ] **tackle** 名 ①（釣り道具などの）道具 ②（ラグビーなどの）タックル 動 ①（問題などに）取り組む ②タックルする
- [ ] **take a look at** ～をちょっと見る
- [ ] **take from** ～から引き出す, 選び取る
- [ ] **take on** （仕事などを）引き受ける, 獲得する
- [ ] **take part in** ～に参加する
- [ ] **take place** 行われる, 起こる
- [ ] **take ～ for granted** ～を当然のことと思う
- [ ] **Tamil Nadu** タミル・ナードゥ《インド共和国の東部にある州》
- [ ] **target** 名 標的, 目的物, 対象 動 的［目標］にする
- [ ] **tariff** 名 関税（率）
- [ ] **task** 名（やるべき）仕事, 職務, 課題 動 仕事を課す, 負担をかける
- [ ] **tax** 名 ①税 ②重荷, 重い負担 動 ① 課税する ②重荷を負わせる
- [ ] **teamwork** 名 チームワーク, 共同作業
- [ ] **temple** 名 ①寺, 神殿 ②こめかみ
- [ ] **tend** 動 ①（～の）傾向がある,（～）しがちである ②面倒を見る, 手入れをする
- [ ] **tension** 名 緊張（関係）, ぴんと張ること
- [ ] **tenure** 名 在職［在任］（期間）
- [ ] **term** 名 ①期間, 期限 ②語, 用語 ③《-s》条件 ④《-s》関係, 仲
- [ ] **territory** 名 ①領土 ②（広い）地域, 範囲, 領域
- [ ] **testament** 名 ①遺言書 ②《the New [Old] –》新約［旧約］聖書
- [ ] **than** 熟 more than ～以上 rather than ～よりむしろ
- [ ] **thank ～ for** ～に対して礼を言う

- [ ] **that** 熟 after that その後 at that time その時 so that ～するために, それで, ～できるように so ～ that … 非常に～なので… there is no doubt that〔that以下〕ということは疑いようがない those that それらの物
- [ ] **the number of** ～の数
- [ ] **the same ～ as [that] …** …と同じ（ような）～
- [ ] **then** 熟 even then その時でさえ
- [ ] **there is no doubt that**〔that以下〕ということは疑いようがない
- [ ] **therefore** 副 したがって, それゆえ, その結果
- [ ] **think of** ～のことを考える
- [ ] **thinker** 名 思想家, 考える人
- [ ] **thinking** 動 think（思う）の現在分詞 way of thinking 物の考え方 名 考えること, 思考 形 思考力のある, 考える
- [ ] **this** 熟 like this このような, こんなふうに
- [ ] **those that** それらの物
- [ ] **those who** ～する人々
- [ ] **though** 接 ①～にもかかわらず, ～だが ②たとえ～でも even though ～であるけれども, ～にもかかわらず 副 しかし
- [ ] **thousand** 熟 hundreds and thousands of 何百, 何千という
- [ ] **threat** 名 おどし, 脅迫
- [ ] **threaten** 動 脅かす, おびやかす, 脅迫する
- [ ] **threatened** 形 脅かされている, 危険が迫っている
- [ ] **throughout** 前 ①～中, ～を通じて ②～のいたるところに 副 初めから終わりまで, ずっと
- [ ] **thus** 副 ①このように ②これだけ ③かくて, だから
- [ ] **tightly** 副 きつく, しっかり, 堅く
- [ ] **time** 熟 at one time ある時には,

131

かつては **at that time** その時　**in time** 間に合って，やがて　**times as … as A** Aの〜倍の…

- **tirelessly** 副 疲れないで，たゆみなく
- **tolerant** 形 寛容な，寛大な
- **toll** 名 犠牲者，死傷者数　**death toll** 死亡者数
- **too 〜 to ...** …するには〜すぎる
- **torch** 名 たいまつ，光明
- **total** 形 総計の，全体の，完全な　名 全体，合計　動 合計する
- **tough** 形 堅い，丈夫な，たくましい，骨の折れる，困難な　**tough on** 《be –》〜に厳しい態度で臨む
- **trace** 名 ①跡　②(事件などの)こん跡　動 たどる，さかのぼって調べる
- **trade** 名 取引，貿易，商業　動 取引する，貿易する，商売する
- **tradition** 名 伝統，伝説，しきたり
- **traditional** 形 伝統的な
- **traditionally** 副 伝統的に，元々は
- **tragic** 形 悲劇の，痛ましい
- **transfer** 動 ①移動する ②移す ③譲渡する　名 ①移動，移送 ②譲渡 ③乗り換え
- **treat** 動 ①扱う ②治療する ③おごる　名 ①おごり，もてなし，ごちそう ②楽しみ
- **treatment** 名 ①取り扱い，待遇 ②治療(法)
- **tremendous** 形 すさまじい，とても大きい
- **tremendously** 副 恐ろしいほどに，大いに
- **trend** 名 トレンド，傾向
- **trial** 名 ①試み，試験 ②苦難 ③裁判　形 試みの，試験の
- **trick** 名 ①策略 ②いたずら，冗談 ③手品，錯覚　動 だます
- **tried** 動 try (試みる)の過去，過去分詞　形 試験済みの，信頼できる
- **troop** 名 群れ，隊　動 ぞろぞろ歩く，群れ[列]をなして進む
- **tropical** 形 熱帯の
- **Trump** 名 《Donald – 》ドナルド・トランプ《アメリカ合衆国第45代大統領（2017-21），1946-》
- **truth** 名 ①真理，事実，本当 ②誠実，忠実さ
- **try hard to** 〜に尽力する
- **trying** 動 try (やってみる)の現在分詞　形 つらい，苦しい，しゃくにさわる
- **tumor** 名 腫瘍，はれ
- **turn out** 集まる，繰り出す
- **turn out to be** 〜という結果になる
- **turning** 動 turn (ひっくり返す)の現在分詞　名 回転，曲がり角
- **turnout** 名 〔選挙の〕投票者(数)，投票率
- **2020 American presidential election** 2020年アメリカ大統領選挙
- **Twitter** 名 ツイッター《ユーザーが140文字以内のテキストなどを投稿してコミュニケーションする，米国Twitter社によるソーシャルネットワーキングサービス》
- **typical** 形 典型的な，象徴的な
- **typically** 副 典型的に，いかにも〜らしく

U

- **ultra-conservative** 形 超保守的な
- **ultraright** 形 極右の
- **unabated** 形 〔力が〕衰えない
- **unalienable** 形 〔権利などが〕譲渡できない，奪うことのできない (= inalienable)
- **unbelievable** 形 信じられない

(ほどの), 度のはずれた

□ **unburden** 動〔～の〕荷を下ろす, 〔悩みを〕打ち明ける

□ **unconstitutional** 形憲法に違反する, 違憲の

□ **undertaking** 動 undertake (引き受ける) の現在分詞 名 (引き受けた) 仕事, 事業

□ **undocumented** 形 ①〔情報が〕文書化されていない, 公開〔登録〕されていない ②密入国の, 不法滞在の

□ **uneducated** 形教養のない, 無学の, 無知の

□ **unemployment** 名失業 (状態)

□ **unexpected** 形思いがけない, 予期しない

□ **unfair** 形不公平な, 不当な

□ **unfairly** 副不当に

□ **unfairness** 名不公正, 不公平

□ **unforgettable** 形忘れられない, 記憶にとどまる

□ **unfortunate** 形不運な, あいにくな, 不適切な

□ **unfortunately** 副不幸にも, 運悪く

□ **union** 名 ①結合, 合併, 融合 ②連合国家 ③《the U-》北部諸州

□ **unique** 形唯一の, ユニークな, 独自の

□ **unit** 名ユニット, 構成単位, 1個, 1人

□ **unite** 動 ①1つにする [なる], 合わせる, 結ぶ ②結束する, 団結する

□ **united** 動 unite (1つにする) の過去, 過去分詞 形団結した, まとまった, 連合した

□ **United Kingdom** 名連合王国, 英国, イギリス《国》

□ **uniter** 名結合 [一体化] させる物 [人], まとめ役

□ **unity** 名単一, 統一

□ **university** 名 (総合) 大学

□ **unjustly** 副不当に

□ **unlike** 形似ていない, 違った 前～と違って

□ **up to** ～まで, ～に至るまで

□ **up to the present** 現在に至るまで

□ **upcoming** 形やがて来る, 来たる

□ **upon** 前 ①《場所・接触》～ (の上) に ②《日・時》～に ③《関係・従事》～に関して, ～について, ～して 副前へ, 続けて

□ **urban** 形都会の, 都市の

□ **used** 動 ①use (使う) の過去, 過去分詞 ②《–to》よく～したものだ, 以前は～であった 形 ①慣れている, 《get [become] –to》～に慣れてくる ②使われた, 中古の

□ **usher** 名案内係 動案内係を務める

V

□ **vaccine** 名ワクチン

□ **value** 名価値, 値打ち, 価格 動評価する, 値をつける, 大切にする

□ **variety** 名 ①変化, 多様性, 寄せ集め ②種類

□ **various** 形変化に富んだ, さまざまの, たくさんの

□ **Vermont** 名バーモント《米国北東部に位置する州》

□ **versus** 前対, ～に対して

□ **vice** 名悪徳, 不道徳 形代理の

□ **victim** 名犠牲者, 被害者

□ **victor** 名勝者, 優勝者

□ **victory** 名勝利, 優勝

□ **view** 熟 point of view 考え方, 視点

□ **violence** 名 ①暴力, 乱暴 ②激しさ

□ **virus** 名ウイルス

- □ **vision** 名①視力 ②先見, 洞察力
- □ **vocal** 形主張する, うるさく求める 名《-s》(楽器演奏に対して)ボーカル
- □ **volunteer** 名志願者, ボランティア 動自発的に申し出る
- □ **vote** 名投票(権), 票決 動投票する, 投票して決める
- □ **voter** 名投票者
- □ **voting** 名〔政治家を選ぶための〕選挙, 投票 形①投票の, 投票に用いる ②投票[議決]権がある
- □ **Voting Rights Act** 《the -》《米》投票権法《1965年8月6日に施行された, 投票時の人種差別を禁じた法》

W

- □ **wait for** ～を待つ
- □ **waiting** 動wait (待つ)の現在分詞 名待機, 給仕すること 形待っている, 仕えている
- □ **wake up** 起きる, 目を覚ます
- □ **wander** 動①さまよう, 放浪する, 横道へそれる ②放心する
- □ **warning** 動warn (警告する)の現在分詞 名警告, 警報
- □ **Washington** 名ワシントン《米国の首都 ; 州》
- □ **Washington D.C.** ワシントンD.C., ワシントン(・コロンビア)特別区《アメリカ合衆国の首都》
- □ **wave** 名①波 ②(手などを)振ること 動①揺れる, 揺らす, 波立つ ②(手などを振って)合図する
- □ **way** 名in the way of ～の邪魔になって, 行く手を塞いで see oneself in a way 自分を～な視点から見る stand in the way 邪魔[妨げ]になる way of life 生き様, 生き方, 暮らし方 way of thinking 物の考え方 way to ～する方法
- □ **wealthy** 形裕福な, 金持ちの

- □ **weapon** 名武器, 兵器 動武装させる, 武器を供給する
- □ **web** 名①クモの巣 ②《the W-》ウェブ(=World Wide Web)
- □ **well** 熟as well なお, その上, 同様に as well as ～と同様に well -ed 《be -》よく[十分に]～された
- □ **well-known** 形よく知られた, 有名な
- □ **West Coast** ウェストコースト, 米国の西海岸
- □ **whenever** 接①～するときはいつでも, ～するたびに ②いつ～しても
- □ **whether** 接～かどうか, ～かまたは…, ～であろうとなかろうと
- □ **white-dominant** 形白人優位の
- □ **who** 熟those who ～する人々
- □ **whole** 形全体の, すべての, 完全な, 満～, 丸～ 《the -》全体, 全部
- □ **whom** 代①誰を[に] ②《関係代名詞》～するところの人, そしてその人を
- □ **wide** 形幅の広い, 広範囲の, 幅が～ある 副広く, 大きく開いて
- □ **widely** 副広く, 広範囲にわたって
- □ **wildfire** 名急速に燃え広がる炎, 山火事
- □ **willingness** 名意欲, 快く～すること
- □ **Wilmington** 名ウィルミントン《デラウェア州最大の都市》
- □ **wing** 名翼, 羽
- □ **winner** 名勝利者, 成功者
- □ **wipe** 動～をふく, ぬぐう, ふきとる 名ふくこと
- □ **Wisconsin** 名ウィスコンシン《米国中西部の最北に位置する州》
- □ **withdraw** 動引っ込める, 取り下げる, (預金を)引き出す
- □ **withdrew** 動withdraw (引っ込める)の過去

☐ **within** 前 ①~の中[内]に, ~の
内部に ②~以内で, ~を越えないで
副 中[内]へ[に], 内部に 名 内部

☐ **witness** 名 ①証拠, 証言 ②目撃
者 動 ①目撃する ②証言する

☐ **wonder** 動 ①不思議に思う, (~
に)驚く ②(~かしらと)思う
wonder if ~ではないかと思う 名
驚き(の念), 不思議なもの

☐ **word** 熟 in other words すなわち,
言い換えれば

☐ **work hard to do** ~するために
懸命に働く

☐ **worker** 名 仕事をする人, 労働者

☐ **working** 動 work(働く)の現在分
詞 形 働く 作業の 実用的な

☐ **world** 熟 all over the world 世界
中に

☐ **worried** 動 worry(悩む)の過去,
過去分詞 形 心配そうな, 不安げな

☐ **worry about** ~のことを心配す
る

☐ **worse** 形 いっそう悪い, より劣っ
た, よりひどい 副 いっそう悪く

☐ **wound** 名 傷 動 ①負傷させる, (感
情を)害する ②wind(巻く)の過去,
過去分詞

☐ **wounded** 形 ①〔戦闘などで〕負
傷した, けがをした ②〔感情などが〕
傷ついた

☐ **wreck** 名 難破(船), 破損 動 難破
する[させる], めちゃめちゃにする

Y

☐ **year** 熟 for ~ years ~年間, ~年
にわたって

Z

☐ **zealot** 名 狂信者, 熱狂者, 政治や宗
教に熱中する人

English Conversational Ability Test
国際英語会話能力検定

● E-CATとは…
英語が話せるようになるための
テストです。インターネット
ベースで、30分であなたの発
話力をチェックします。

www.ecatexam.com

● iTEP®とは…
世界各国の企業、政府機関、アメリカの大学
300校以上が、英語能力判定テストとして採用。
オンラインによる90分のテストで文法、リー
ディング、リスニング、ライティング、スピー
キングの5技能をスコア化。iTEP®は、留学、就
職、海外赴任などに必要な、世界に通用する英
語力を総合的に評価する画期的なテストです。

www.itepexamjapan.com

ラダーシリーズ
The Kamala Harris Story カマラ・ハリス・ストーリー

2021年7月4日　第1刷発行

著　者　西海コエン

英文編集　マイケル・ブレーズ

発行者　浦　晋亮

発行所　**IBCパブリッシング株式会社**
　　　　〒162-0804 東京都新宿区中里町29番3号
　　　　菱秀神楽坂ビル9F
　　　　Tel. 03-3513-4511　Fax. 03-3513-4512
　　　　www.ibcpub.co.jp

印　刷　株式会社シナノパブリッシングプレス
装　丁　伊藤 理恵

Printed in Japan
ISBN978-4-7946-0664-8